People do not believe lies because they have to, but because they want to

(Malcolm Muggeridge)

A Brief History Of Lies
First Published 2010 Updated 2013, 2021
Published by Footsteps Press
ISBN: 978-1-908867-08-7

A Brief History of Lies
Updated

A survey of a wicked, irreverent, serious, harmful,
cruel and enjoyable (for some) side of human civilization.

Including quotes on lies and lying (good, bad and
indifferent) from famous people down the ages
who should know better.

By
Daniel Benshana

with
Calvin Innes

Without lies humanity would perish of despair and boredom.
(Anatole France)

Each day a few more lies eat into the seed with which we are born, little institutional lies from the print of newspapers, the shock waves of television, and the sentimental cheats of the movie screen.
(Norman Mailer)

Contents

Clever liars give details, but the cleverest don't.
(Anonymous)

Thank You

This book would not be what it is without the editorial
assistance of Polly East and Jenna Pascoe.
I would not be what I am without the help and
assistance of my mother, Shänne Sands.

To the rulers of the state then, if to any, it belongs of right to use falsehood, to
deceive either enemies or their own citizens, for the good of the state: and no one
else may meddle with this privilege.
(Plato)

Why do we lie? The answer may seem obvious to you because you know why you have, and even when you haven't quite known the answer, it was never important enough for you to fret over; especially when you got away with it. But in the very obviousness of this answer we all may be missing the deeper, underlying reasons. In a very interesting conversation I had with the respected Oxford anthropologist Bruce Corrie, he touched upon the 'natural order of things' (in terms of evolution) and how everything we create and do, is a reflection of Nature. So the question become, 'What is the evolutionary advantage in being able to lie?'

The answer to this also seems obvious, until you ask yourself what the evolutionary advantage might be in lying to someone you love?

This short book looks at some of the most recent research done by psychologist, behaviourists, sociologists and security services and tries to shed some fascinating light upon the subject. Suggesting that lies go deeper than we ever expected before, because of our ability to lie to ourselves; and that what may have been a survival mechanism has not only come to be used inappropriately but for some becomes, if not a way-of-life, then the way life works.

It is always the best policy to speak the truth--unless, of course,
you are an exceptionally good liar.
(H. L. Mencken)

I DON'T KNOW WHAT IT IS...
THERE'S JUST SOMETHING I DON'T TRUST ABOUT HIM!

Categories of Lies

or
Mangoes and Onions

Before psychologists created themselves, the only people who talked about lies were philosophers, when they discussed ethics, and religious people on their way to becoming saints.

Everyone who wrote and thought about lies quoted each other regularly over the centuries. St. Jerome from St.Origen, St.Origen from Plato, who quoted Socrates:

"If ... falsehood is disgraceful and useless to God, to men it is sometimes useful, if only it is used as a stimulant or a medicine..."
(Plato, third book of The Republic. Not my translation)

Another saint, St.Augustine, devoted two whole treatises to the topic. 'On Lying', and twenty-seven years later he wrote 'Against Lies.' He identified eight kinds of lie:

Lies in religious teaching.
Lies that harm others and help no one.
Lies that harm others and help someone.
Lies told for the pleasure of lying.
Lies told to "please others during conversation."
Lies that harm no one yet help someone.

And, after all, what is a lie? 'Tis but the truth in masquerade.
(Lord Byron)

Lies that harm no one and save life.

Lies that harm no one and save someone's "purity."

This list was the first of many, many more and I have a suspicion that ideas of purity, in one form or another, underline much of the comment made about lies, liars and lying down the centuries.

Surprisingly, psychologists have only been seriously analyzing lies and why we use them since the 1980s. They divide lies into many different categories and choose differing categories and place differing emphasis on their categories. Much like any of us they have a set of ideas about lies - which ones we should be angry about, which ones we feel we should expect, and which ones we should divorce over. We all know what lies are, and we all frown on them to a certain degree, but we all find a regular use for them. For the most part this book is all about those uses. And you can criticise those uses as being abuses of the truth if you wish to, no one will mind and I can't hear you.

But I do wonder why the 1980s, the decade of rampant Thatcherite monetarism and glasnost (openness) brought about a deeper study of lies? Perhaps because there is a growing awareness that being human is not something you just accept being, but being one analyzes.

Here are some more categories, many of which St.Augustine did not think of, itemized by people who have thought a lot about lying (in the nicest sense) and, as far as I know, are still alive and have no ambitions to become saints:

A lie can run around the world before the truth can get it's boots on.
(James G Watt)

Ambiguity:-	This is a deliberate attempt to mislead through the misuse of logic and the talent for oratory. Syllogisms can be misused in this way. It is also a mainstay of comedy, where we can recognise it instantly.
Bluff:-	This is the pretence to possess a power or an intention which one does not actually have. Bluffing is an act of deception which is accepted and indeed expected as a tactic in games and every other walk of life. Hollywood wouldn't exist without it as all films are a type of deception.
Brazen:-	A brazen lie is one which is told when it is obvious to the teller and to those listening, that it is an untruth. For example, a child who has chocolate all around his mouth who denies that he has eaten any chocolate is a brazen liar. In the present climate anyone saying, I am a trustworthy banker would also fit this category especially if the banker had chocolate around his mouth.
Conceit:-	Lying to oneself. Whole communities can lie to themselves.
Contextual:-	These lies take the truth out of context thereby making someone believe it isn't the truth. So saying sarcastically, "Oh sure! Your sister gets pregnant, and you blame me," would fit this category if the speaker was responsible.

A lie told often enough becomes the truth.
(Lenin)

Dissembling:-	Presenting facts in a way that is literally true, but intentionally misleading.
Emergency:-	Years ago I knew an Irishman who was adopted and we found his birth certificate. Finding out the names of his parents when he was over 30, he said if he ever met his mother he would kill her. He would have been somewhat happier not to have known about his birth certificate. The truth can hurt.
Equivocate:-	Pure and simple evasion of the truth, which is taught in a few walks of life.
Exaggeration:-	People don't think this is a very serious lie in most cases but for myself, saying this is the best country in the world when you know about thirty countries are saying the same thing with some justice encourages ignorant nationalism. But what would I know?
Fabrication: -	A fabrication is saying something without actually knowing whether or not it is true.
Fraud:-	Criminal fraud occurs when the victim loses (has stolen) a valuable possession with (apparently) no benefit to themselves but this is actually an intentional deception
Gender Specific:-	Lies women tell men: "You're so big." ; "This is my true hair color." ; " The earth moved." etc. Lies men tell women: "I am not lost."; "That looks good on you." ; "I am sterile, I don't need a condom." etc.

Falsehood is invariably the child of fear in one form or another.
(Alistair Crowley)

Hoax:-	Anything that happens for April 1st reasons.
Institutional:-	It was Ignatius Loyola who said that if the Church told him black was white then black was white. Loyola's words are a perfect example of the dangers of institutions trying to change reality for their own benefit.
Jargonese:-	It has to be said that when the Law was all in Latin it militated against the general public who did not understand a word of it. It is the same today in India where the Law is in English. This lack of understanding supports those 'in-the-know' and extends to many spheres of activity beyond the Law. (Quite literally beyond the Law in some countries)
Jest:-	Usually seen as a joke, this is a form of teasing intended to be enjoyed by everyone within earshot. "England has the best cricketers!", has quite different meanings when said in a Surrey pub as to when it is said in Mumbai.
Linguistic:-	We don't only lie with words, but sometimes there is a deliberate methodology within grammar and syntax to confuse and blind. Oxymorons are a standard example (revolutionary government, wise human-being, etc.)

Good lies need a leavening of truth to make them palatable.
(William Mcilvanney)

Noble:-	A noble lie would normally cause discord if it were uncovered, but it assists the community when it is given. It maintains law and order which helps the rulers. Sometimes also called Paternalistic Lie, but note the male attribution. Nowhere did I find a maternalistic lie defined.
Omission:-	A husband may tell his wife he was out at a store, which is true, but lie by omitting the fact that he also visited his mistress. It may not be much of a lie, but some people would have you believe it's a sin.
Pathological:-	According to recent studies people who exhibit this condition have brains incapable of differentiating between the truth and fiction because of the way their synapses are connecting in the front of their brains.
Perjury:-	A crime.
Propaganda:-	Information is always propagandist and contains bias but sometimes this bias is intended. Advertisements are an obvious example. Years ago a breakfast cereal ran adverts challenging people to eat three portions in one go, masking the fact that for cost reasons the size of the portions was being reduced.

Any fool can tell the truth, but it requires a man of some sense
to know how to lie well.
(Samuel Butler)

Relationship:-	See the chapter on Conspiracies (I know but the list is there for a reason of emphasis not to make you believe every relationship is a potential lie.)
To Children:-	See the chapter on children.
Vindictive:-	These are aimed at harming someone, a group, organization or country. Whilst thought among the worst kind of lies, lies given to one's lover are considered worse, at least by the lover.
White:-	A white lie would cause no argument if it were found out but be careful, a white lie in one culture may be perjury in another.

This list, though more informative than Augustine's is by no means extensive. There are far longer lists, but I think we can get the drift. Human beings can lie about anything, anytime, in any situation, for any reason.

It's a skill.

Mostly we should expect them (especially if we live in Argentina apparently).

The lies we find hardest to take are not those which are just deliberate but those that are also vindictive and planned. But beware, we are all different and some people hate the innocent, off-the-cuff white lie just as much as the nasty, selfish one. Their emphasis is not so much on what kind of lie they are told, but on the absence of truth itself. They are in a minority.

Dr. Leonard Saxe, a polygraph expert and professor of psychology at Brandeis University, observes,

---

Don't lie if you don't have to.
(Leo Szilard)

GREAT IDEA JENKINS...
THOSE BABIES ARE REALLY
FLYING OFF THE SHELVES!

"Lying has long been a part of everyday life. We couldn't get through the day without being deceptive."

As psychologists delve deeper into the details of lying they are finding that lying is a surprisingly common and complex phenomenon. Hence all the lists.

Is lying really a condition of being human? In a 1996 study, Dr.Bella DePaulo, a visiting professor at the University of California, Santa Barbara and her colleagues had 147 people between the ages of 18 and 71 keep a diary of their lies over the course of a week. They didn't just trust them to know when they lied (would you?).

He who is not very strong in memory should not meddle with lying.
(Michel De Montaigne)

"We had a 90 minute session explaining the whole study to them, including how we defined lies. We also encouraged them to list the lie, if they were not sure it counted as a lie; then my co-authors and I read through them all to be sure they qualified."

Most people, she found, lie once or twice a day— almost as often as they snack from the refrigerator or brush their teeth. Both men and women in the community sample (excluding the college students) lie in approximately a fifth of their social exchanges lasting 10 or more minutes; over the course of a week they deceive about 30 percent of those with whom they interact one-on-one. Furthermore, some types of relationships, such as those between parents and teens, are virtual magnets for deception:

"College students lie to their mothers in one out of two conversations."

The college students lied in one-third of their social interactions. It is interesting to note the difference and one wonders if college students lie a little else because their whole world is about facts, clarity and thoughtful opinion. DePaulo does not include pleasantries or polite equivocations such as "I'm fine, thanks" in the definition of what constitutes a lie.

Dr.Saxe points out that most of us receive conflicting messages about lying. Although we're socialized from the time we can speak to believe that it is always better to tell the truth, in reality society often encourages and rewards deception. Showing up late for an early morning meeting at work, it is best not to admit that you overslept.

"You're punished far more than you would be if you lie and say

---

I detest the man who hides one thing in the depth of his heart and speaks forth another.
(Homer)

you were stuck in traffic, moreover, lying is integral to many occupations. Think how often we see lawyers constructing theories to support their client's case or reporters posing to get good stories."

Dr.Saxe believes that anyone under enough pressure, or given enough incentive, will lie.

"Lying is a function of social interaction. Lies are constructed/ maintained to foster social interaction and, if we want to reduce the frequency of lies, we have to make it possible for people to tell the truth -- particularly about foibles/negative behavior "

As shown in a study published in the 'Journal of Personality and Social Psychology', Dr. DePaulo and Dr. Deborah A. Kashy, of Texas A&M University, frequent liars tend to be manipulative and Machiavellian, not to mention overly concerned with the impression they make on others. Liars ...

"... don't always fit the stereotype of caring only about themselves. Further research reveals that extroverted, sociable people are slightly more likely to lie, and that self-confidence and physical attractiveness have been linked to an individual's skill at lying when under pressure."

This last observation accords with the accepted belief that physical beauty impresses people and the more beautiful you are the more inclined people are to believe you.

We lie to each other to cover up the truth, or the fact that we don't know anything, or to make ourselves look better. When I was 9 I told my school friends I was a black belt in karate so they wouldn't bully me. This was a useless (and brazen) lie as everyone knew I was nothing of the sort.

The visionary lies to himself, the liar only to others.
(Franklin D. Roosevelt)

Useless lies are why we start lying at the age of 4 so that by the time we are 18 we know how to avoid making an obvious lie. Obvious lies are left behind with childhood toys ... unless you meet with someone who has heard it all before and can see right through you!

Most adults don't set out to lie; it's a reflex action given the situation and the people they are interacting with. There are some people who will lie to anyone and those who just lie to you and me - but who would never think of lying to someone with the power to arrest them.

We do train some people to lie well and to everyone. Although we probably all have that aptitude it can certainly be enhanced. Generally they work for the CIA, etc. in the United Kingdom we have MI5, MI6 and probably an MI7 and MI8 though who will admit to organizations existing that are supposed to be invisible?

The sexes are pretty evenly divided on who are the better liars. Ability is, in fact, not a gender issue. But here are some obvious liars I put before you, for you to consider:

All the leaders of the world there have ever been, have lied, though they didn't lie all the time and didn't lie to everyone all the time. But whoever they were, are and will be, they lied and will lie. What makes them good leaders is their knowing just when to lie, about what, to whom and for how long and to always have a ready excuse if the lie is uncovered.

Every crook that has ever lived or will ever live, lies. They never steal, kill, plot or plan. They are just like everyone else in the world except they got caught.

Baron Münchausen reportedly told people that he had

Someone who always has to lie discovers that every one of his lies is true.
(Elias Canetti)

travelled to the Moon, ridden cannonballs, and escaped from a swamp by pulling himself out by his own hair. Münchausen Syndrome is a disorder in which someone feigns illness in order to get attention. Münchausen Syndrome By Proxy is a disorder in which a caregiver (usually the mother) fakes or induces illness in their child or in another person in their care in order to gain attention and sympathy. You have to be a really good liar to have disorders named after you.

Children's book writers who make it seem there is a place where fairies, goblins, witches and orphans all live a merry-go-round happy-ever-after existence. What whoppers!

Train timetable compilers.

The rich, no wholly truthful person ever made millions of anything.

Advertisers.

Actors whose whole lives are taken up with pretending. (I am told 'pretend' is not lying. What do you think?)

I am certain you can think of many more.

And then with all this lying to others we must address the far more relevant and often harder to detect kind of lies. Those we tell ourselves. Because at the heart of believing others' lies is the hope, desire, wish that they were and are telling us the truth. Because in the world we would prefer to live in, what they say to us, would never be lies.

Lying to oneself is something we all do. "I am not really overweight."; "I can get there on time."; "I am really funny."; "I am the most handsome person in the world because my mother told me so."

Some self given lies get dangerous, but in the main it

Some truth there was, but dash'd and brew'd with lies, To please the fools, and puzzle all the wise.
(John Dryden)

is just a way of making sure we don't get too upset at ageing. And it helps writers enormously because we can kid ourselves into believing anything we write is worth reading ... it is also a great way for hack writers to consider themselves something better than they are. In addition it helps editors who all want to be good writers and so very rarely can be because they have to stop being editors first. We are habituated to self-given lies, a theme I shall return to.

For the most part it is not easy to recognise a really good liar which is why a great deal of time and effort has been expended on lie-detectors and considerable credence given to training observers to watch suspects for their lies.

It is not the aim of this little book to overview every situation in which people lie. I will limit it from now to a few places such as politics, business and war, and relationships because the same 'kinds' of lying crop up in every sphere of life. And I retread these well known areas that others have written reams about for two reasons. To look at how evolution works in these areas and to look at how lying to ourselves allows us to plug-into 'universal' lies.

But first a question.

When does this habit of lying all start?

Great talker, great liar.
(French Proverb)

In Children

or
Machiavellian Intelligence

Lying would appear to be part of everyone's life (some even make it a lifestyle) and it begins very young. Modern child psychologists tell us that people of average intelligence start to lie when they are about 4 years old, of higher intelligence when they are about 3 years old.

They term this commencement of lying in the young 'Machiavellian Intelligence'. Presumably because Niccolò Machiavelli has something of a reputation for promoting craftiness. In point of fact he was just being honest about power politics as he saw it in his time, and had he seen any leaders getting power, extending their boundaries and ruling their populations securely, by being honest, he would have promoted honesty.

Dr. Victoria Talwar, of Montreal's McGill University says that lying is related to intelligence. Presumably this is why so many of us think we marry idiots.

A child's ability to tell us the Emperor has no clothes on has long been an endearing facet in some children. They say it as they see it which is a facility we don't appreciate in adults (but more of that later).

However, lying is an advanced skill because we learn it. Much of lying is no more than habit. We don't learn how to tell the truth. Well some of us do!

Nobody speaks the truth when there's something they must have.
(Elizabeth Bowen)

When a child lies they actually know the truth so they know they are lying, they have put together a falsehood which is still based on the way the world around them works, and they have the self- belief that they can sell their lie to those they are lying to. Therefore, lying demands both 'advanced cognitive development' as well as 'social skills'. Which is a lot for a four year old let me tell you.

This isn't true of all lies, some are told because of fear and other emotions. But maybe the time, place and situation in which we tell our first ever lie - possibly long forgotten to us as we age - marks out our pattern of lying.

I could never lie to my mother and get away with it because she saw it written on my forehead every time.

Apparently honesty doesn't require the same abilities presumably because we don't care as much if people believe us or not when we tell the truth, but we do when we tell them a lie. I wonder if this is some kind of 'affirmation' exercise. Since we can be certain ourselves of the truth of the matter, we have a certainty that cannot be shaken. But since lies are set in sand we need to know they won't slip away from us, and the agreement (spoken or not) of those we lie to sets the lie in firm foundations in our minds. A lie accepted by others has a reality of its own. An affirmed lie like this has the strength of the truth.

If there were a branch of psychology called Machiavellian Logic that strand of thought would certainly fit into it. Basically we have to 'catch out' a liar, but we don't assume in our language that we have to 'catch' the truth at all. We assume lies are the exception, the deviation from the mean-point.

For my part getting up seems not so easy by half as lying.

(Thomas Hood)

"It's a developmental milestone," Dr. Talwar has concluded. That is, it is learned from our surroundings and how we try to deal with them.

A test the psychologists did to fix on four as the age this milestone is reached went something like this. Developmental work was done with children up to the age of four to see if they could save the princess doll from the wicked witch. Most when asked outright where she was hiding told the adults straight away but by the age of four the kids started to point in places where she was not hiding so as to help save her. Bright kids lied a year earlier. Of course the really, really bright kids looked at the adults and said,

"Let's stop pissing about with dolls and talk about police corruption."

Interestingly they don't say if some of the children refused to answer. Presumably you have to have a certain degree of bravery to stay silent and perhaps we don't develop that amount of courage for a few more years, or perhaps we lie at four on behalf of the princess as long as we don't have any adverse consequences to ourselves. At any rate it shows the possibility that lying and fear go hand-in-hand. We wouldn't want to be in the clutches of the wicked witch (until we cannot avoid it and start paying taxes) and we don't want the princess doll to fall into her clutches either.

It also proves bright people are better at lying than average people because they have one year's more practice. So wherever you find high intelligence you may well find first rate liars and if you don't, I think you've found integrity.

On a deeper level the child has empathized with the princess' plight and doesn't want anything bad to happen

---

If one cannot invent a really convincing lie, it is often better to stick to the truth.

(Angela Thirkell)

to her. It would seem from this that the first kind of lies we can tell, are based upon a child's growing idea of compassion. Maybe they can lie about where the doll is earlier but they don't actually 'care' about what happens to her before they are four or so. It would be interesting to know if the same response was found if they used a cow hiding from a farmer come to send it to the abattoir, and if it was found to be the same why that compassion disappears in most adults, whereas saving a princess (another human being) does not. This assumes that a child of three or four knows that a doll represents a real human being, or that the doll is in some way 'real' to them, which I think is a fair assumption.

Of course there is something in this example that is not learnt. The child is protecting the princess doll from a threat. In a world where threats abound this kind of response is both sensible and community orientated in that the child is protecting someone else which is what the child expects others to do for them. There may be a kind of symbiotic logic here in that we lie hoping someone would lie for us in the same situation. Lies in this case are almost an instinctive form of protection. As we shall see although many lies are to protect the individual there are others that one may assume anyone would use in the same situation, and so carry this variant form of community benefit with them.

Take another study. A number of two and three year-old children were seated in an empty room and told not to look at a toy placed on a table behind them. The researcher left and secretly watched the kids by video returning to the room a few minutes later. Ninety per cent of the children looked at the toy, and the majority, about 64%, tried to conceal their

---

If you want to be thought a liar, always tell the truth.
(Logan Pearsall Smith)

peeking. One-third lied outright, saying they did not peek, while the other third didn't answer the question, pretending not to hear it, (bravery issues).

At this age, wishes and imagination often get in the way of what is real. Sometimes a three year old will start to tell a story, and you will hear it start to get out of hand as s/he adds bits and pieces to fit the growing or incomplete ideas in their head. Three year olds are generally poor liars because they fail to lie appropriately. They do not consider that their listener will actually think about either their statements or their intentions in making them. As a result, they tend to lie at the wrong time or place, or neglect to think about other important facts, such as covering their tracks to conceal the lies. The same kind of process appears in people lying on the hoof and trying to keep the lie going over a prolonged period of interrogation. It is a fact that throughout our lives we like our lies to be quick and easy. Said and dead. Except they never are.

By age four, children know the difference between telling the truth and lying — and they know it's wrong to lie. So, generally, they are truthful, and when they are not it's obvious. But they also become more proficient at lying because they're more cognitively capable of taking into account the listener's belief in their statement.

With children aged four to six, they found that the children were better at resisting the temptation to peek. But those who did look were more apt to lie about it. Videotapes showed another important difference in the older children: After they looked at the toy, they didn't look very happy. They did, however, change their facial expression once the

---

researcher came back, they literally "put on a face." So at age six we are ready to play poker and become actors.

As one five year old said, "You should never tell a lie because the brains inside grown-ups' heads are so smart they always find out." Cute kid, s/he will be a lawyer.

A more sophisticated level of lying emerges between the ages of six and eight. Children can now understand something like, "John wants his mother to think he feels bad about his grandmother not coming to visit." At this stage, it's not just the content of the lie, but the motive or attitude of the speaker, that can be doubted as well.

Looking ahead to ages ten and eleven, most children become able liars. The big difference at this stage is that parents and teachers are no longer seduced by the sound of a child's voice, the innocent look on their face, or an outlandish alibi (now I know). This plays out in adults because a good looking person is more likely to encourage trust in their listeners or readers.

What reasons do we have, outside of child psychologists' experiments, for lying?

Are we hoping we can all base our lives on the same assumptions? (One religion for the whole world!)

Because we don't like people not believing what we believe?

Because we feel foolish?

Because we don't like trouble?

Because we benefit socially and materially from them?

Because we enjoy it?

It is Homer who has chiefly taught other poets the art of telling lies skilfully.
(Aristotle)

Whatever the answers once we have learned to lie, our understanding of the use and power of lies is obvious when they work. And we work on making them work. They go from being a skill, to being a tool.

Dr.John M. Grohol observes that this first lying in the young is not to be malicious, but rather it is children manipulating their environment. For environment read parents, other kids, teachers and especially grandmother who has the tastiest sweets but never visits.

This manipulation has a pay-off. When we lie we get away with something, we get satisfaction, we don't get punished, we don't get bullied and the witch doesn't get the princess. It is a game-play with a positive benefit to the liar if they succeed even though it's a negative activity.

This means good liars probably become mathematicians, which is the only other activity humans have found that gets a positive from a negative.

Actually, lying is thought to be an 'evolutionary psychological process' (something the species needs) because lying is even seen in apes who, in experiments, used sign language to "blame" something they did on another animal when they were confronted with their naughtiness. This might be stretching it a bit as we don't know the ape equivalent of owning up. They may never do it. Maybe we evolved to tell the truth from an animal that always lied. Who knows?

But children are not silly. They know when adults lie - and copy them. And children are more adept at facial queues than adults because their continued existence depends on them knowing they are looking at someone who wants them to live. Not something all parents want all the time. As Dr.

It is easier to gather up a bag of loose feathers than to round up or head off a single lie.

(Anonymous)

Grohol says,

"the truth is, kids learn by modeling and learning from the behavior they see in their environment."

Starting young we eventually lie in about 1 in 5 social interactions. (Or 5 in 5 of sexual interactions.) It's a normal, everyday occurrence many of us take for granted, but people who are honest and expect honesty in others are maddened by this fact and end up getting far less sex than the rest of us. Because of child psychologists we now know not to blame the little apes as its not their fault they lie — it makes complete sense in some situations to do so. You can now spend a lot of time differentiating between the types of lies we all tell, and which ones are thought to be de-rigueur and which ones are thought to be plain awful.

Children will boast, claim things and tell stories as a form of power play with their peers. This natural form of lying becomes something much more serious because you learn one crucial fact ... people believe lies. You learn the lies they won't accept and you learn the ones they will. If the child is father and mother to the adult, this is a very dangerous lesson. But then adults don't go around telling other adults that they have a new red fire-engine in their house with a real engine in it. No, with the adult mind comes the sophistication to lie about the big issues.

But let me be honest here, although the adult goes on to lie about different things, and in different situations, the basis of why they lie stays the same. They lie about things that matter to them or the people they are lying to. It is never worth lying about something no one really bothers or cares

---

It takes a wise man to handle a lie, a fool had better remain honest.
(Norman Douglas)

about. I mean ... where's the fun?

Dr.Frances Stott, Professor of Child Development at the Erikson Institute in Chicago explains it this way as we grow older:-

"Children will lie for many of the same reasons adults do: to avoid punishment, gain an advantage in a social interaction, protect against an unwanted consequence, and to boost self-esteem. Like adults, sometimes they lie to demonstrate power, to maintain privacy, or to protect a friend. When a child lies, they are essentially trying to change a situation, to reconstruct things the way they want them to be at the time. Planned, well-thought-out lies, are something adults seem to practice more readily than children."

When we hear different people saying different things about the same subject it may not be because they are actually lying, just that none of them actually knows the truth. If someone told someone 4,000 years ago the Earth was flat, we can't say they were lying; just that they were mistaken. After all, to all intents and purposes, it looked flat to them. Perception anticipates belief. Of course then belief takes over and shapes perception.

There eventually comes a realization that you won't always get away with a lie so there is a time and place for lying if you don't want to be known as a pathological liar or fantasist. Lies are not there to distance yourself from the community. Quite the opposite. Many are simply given to forestall an argument, for an 'easy-life'.

As we grow we learn this. But parents share some blame because they teach lying. As much as the studies show there is an hereditary role, nurture cannot be forgotten. We can learn the worst habits very quickly when we are young

---

All men are born truthful and die liars.
(Luc de Clapiers)

and they are almost impossible to break. The relationship between the lies we learn and the ability to lie we inherit is probably comparable to xenophobia in its myriad forms. We are born with an ability to become attached to those around us and hence be wary of strangers, but we are taught to hate strangers and the strange.

Here are some of the peccadilloes we are taught, and which we pass on to our children without the slightest hesitation, in fact we believe them to be enjoyable lies. Even a normal part of childhood because they were part of our childhoods.

1. Adults' insistence that the Tooth Fairy, Santa Claus, Little People etc, exist is a pervasive lie in many, many cultures. Even when it isn't specifically these it is a bogey-man of some kind, a ghost of some kind, a mythical being of some kind. The origins of these beings vary according to legend and culture. Parents carry on insisting they exist for as long as the children will believe them as a part of the role play of childhood. When their non-existence is revealed it is the beginning of depression and a career in Hollywood writing Christmas feel-good films.

Every government is run by liars and nothing they say should be believed.
(I. F. Stone)

2. It is apparently difficult to talk to children about vagina's and penises. It's even difficult for children to think about their parents having vaginas and penises and it is a wonderful part of modern society that in some families at last, there is either no penis or no vagina. These families don't have to tell children about sex and birth ... they can just tell their children they were chosen. The ones left who still have to tell their children about sex will invent things to stop from having to tell the sexual facts. Besides, storks and miracles are the way all women wish children came into the world, so it doesn't actually seem to be lying more like wishful thinking.

3. All children have the beauty of babies, the wonder of toddlers, the handsomeness of growing up. But we don't leave it there. We tell them they are film stars. Which is a terrible thing to tell them when you see the disastrous lives film stars have. It's almost wishing them to unhappiness. Some children really are the most beautiful in the world. The rest of us will have to treasure the lies our parents told us. Some lies are worth treasuring.

I am a lie who always speaks the truth.
(Jean Cocteau)

4. We want our children to live forever. In fact we want to live forever but we will tell our children versions of 'you will live 100 years', knowing we have no idea whether or not it will be true. This is more wishful thinking and when the child is sick of cancer at 45 or for some other reason doesn't make 100, they won't blame their parents for lying to them, they will have long ago forgotten it.

OH YES OF COURSE, HE'S A VERY
FRIENDLY DOG.. GREAT WITH KIDS!

He who permits himself to tell a lie once, finds it much easier to do it
a second and a third time till at length it becomes habitual.
(Thomas Jefferson)

5.   Divorcing parents do, according to the psychologists, divorce their children from their parenting duties. It is never going to be quite the same again. Children are divorced from schools, and often homes and have new adults to contend with. The Children's Society report 2009 showed in the United Kingdom some 23% have stepfathers. And remember the children will have to live with this for 100 years, without the back up of Santa Claus and realize this is where sex leads the most beautiful adults in the world.

The terrible thing about lying to children in this way is that they always find out the truth ... and then two things happen. On the one hand, they won't trust everything you say anymore. On the other they recall how comfortable, and lovely life was when they were living in the belief that the lies of the people who were looking after them and supposed to love them the most, were true. So they confuse love and lying, happiness and lying, ease of living and lying ... you get the picture. Other children who see their parents lying to get on have an even worse world view.

And it goes on to pervade every facet of what we do.

The rest of this little book is about adult lying. You know what adults are ... the consequences of children.

There is nothing so easy as by sheer volubility to deceive a common crowd or an uneducated congregation.
(St. Jerome)

In Adults

or
Dishonesty As Policy

Well obviously, adults learn to lie from watching their 4 year old children with child psychologists.

The other way they learn is from embarrassment, which is what clothes are for - if the Adam and Eve story is indicative of anything. That said, we should recognize all clothes are theatre and when they are not covering up our embarrassment, they are saying something to the world that we want the world to believe about us. Whether or not it is true. Maybe all lies are in some way saying the same kinds of thing. A mask that we think protects us.

As we have seen, until recently lying was not deeply studied by psychologists and those who did deal with it, being as we saw mostly ethicists or saints, saw it as a problem to be solved, a vice to be resisted, except in very rare and specific instances. Lying and ethics have a relationship because truth-telling and ethics have a relationship. Because human intellect has a relationship with ethics. Indeed, Ethics have become the defining characteristic of humanity.

However if lying is in any way an evolutionary development, if we think about it, there may actually be a point to lying and that evolutionary point may be the residual reason why we continue to lie so much despite our desire for truth and in contradiction to most ethical thought.

In our country the lie has become not just a moral category but a pillar of the State.
(Alexander Solzhenitsyn)

Freud wrote a little about lying, and the Encyclopaedia of Psychology, published in 1984, mentions lies only in a brief entry about detecting them. Detection though, may be the real point of them!

Human beings have a particular penchant for believing in wonders. To know that when you were lied to was a very happy time of your life full of fairies, saints, fauns and magical worlds, leads one to wish to be lied to again in the hope of recapturing that rare experience of wonder mixed with warmth. Happiness and security. Which is a nice idea but what about people with insecure memories of childhood. Lies work in their lives too.

The ability to lie is obviously part of us, maybe dissemble would be a more acceptable word, but the question we have to ask is what caused that ability to exist in our brains in the first place and has it grown stronger for a reason?

The obvious answer is that dissembling can save life, yours or someone else's. There was a theory that fainting was part of our make-up because, rather like the possum, passing out and being inert in the face of danger (say a bear coming to find a meal) enhances survival rates by making us motionless in some non-specified undergrowth. In other words if you can't outrun a predator fainting may be your next best option. In the same way learning to camouflage not only our bodies but our intentions, aims and meaning, gives us an advantage if we feel our interests, and someone else's interests are in some kind of antagonism or danger. Wishing to spare someone pain is not an example of this, but business competitors lying to each other, would be.

Unusually for inherent abilities lying helps not just

When lying, be emphatic and indignant, thus behaving like your children.
(William Feather)

the liar but the lied-to as well. For if we are evolved to lie as a survival mechanism, we are all forewarned to expect lies from each other. This makes us evaluate people's 'true' intentions. This makes us ask, what advantage do they have in lying to us and what would they lose, if anything, if they told us the truth, in any given situation? This means that in a world of lies the astute and linguistically sophisticated, the story-teller and the realist, the crooked and the honest are in a continuous war with each other and in some ways this benefits the mind because we have to sort through a vast array of information to disinter the truth in the face of the many forms a lie can take. However it should be noted that continual lying of the kind we all encounter and give-out, doesn't benefit society at all. There are those who argue lies of lesser kinds smooth over human relations, but actually we would all do much better to have the truth out in the open and not have to wait a century for the historians to uncover it.

The honest person who hates prevarication and tells it as it is, is usually a very unhappy person in today's world since they are in a minority. It is very difficult for them to deal with people who do not match their truthful outlook on situations, who dissemble and mask their true intentions towards them. This is especially true when they have to do any kind of business and interact on a professional level. We all know about the promises that are not kept. People who are used to lying and being lied to, do much better in organizations of all kinds than people who are honest. An honest person in today's society is really a round peg trying to fit into a square hole.

I would dodge, not lie, in the national interest.
(Larry M Speakes)

This is particularly interesting to me in the world of the arts where it is well known that modern movements entail a heady mixture of flattery, self-interest, hidden agendas and money to persuade other people of their merit and talent. Any individual artist meeting with these movements and adversely criticizing them, is rubbished, ignored and silenced through neglect of their own work. This happens across the board in almost every sphere of human activity and in every generation. It is the reason why many 'great artists' are picked up by succeeding generations and called 'ahead of their time'. They could have been just as popular in their lifetimes but they didn't play the lie game.

But some brains have taken lying to whole new regions of expertise. We call them pathological liars and until recently they were deeply denigrated as people who just lied and lied and lied. New studies show there is something far more interesting going on. So interesting that is the reason why 'evolutionary' actually is a pertinent description of some lying.

A recent study (2005) by the University of Southern California headed by Dr.Adrian Raine and Yaling Yang, has found the first potential proof of structural brain abnormalities in people who habitually lie, cheat and manipulate others.

Previous research shows that the prefrontal cortex (the area of the brain where we learn ethical behavior) is very active when normal people lie. Dr. Adrian Raine's team provided evidence that this area of the brain in pathological liars (those who cannot differentiate at all between truth and falsehood) is structurally different.

In human relationships, kindness and lies are worth a thousand truths.
(Graham Greene)

108 volunteers were recruited from the Los Angeles' temporary employment pool. A series of psychological tests and interviews placed 12 in the category of people who had a history of repeated lying (11 men, one woman); 16 who exhibited signs of antisocial personality disorder but not pathological lying (15 men, one woman); and 21 who were normal controls (15 men, six women).

"We looked for things like inconsistencies in their stories about occupation, education, crimes and family background ... Pathological liars can't always tell truth from falsehood and contradict themselves in an interview. They are manipulative and they admit they prey on people. They are very brazen in terms of their manner, but very cool when talking about this."

After they were categorized, the researchers used Magnetic Resonance Imaging to explore structural brain differences between the groups. The liars had significantly more "white matter" and slightly less "gray matter" than those they were measured against.

Specifically, liars had a 25.7 % increase in prefrontal white matter compared to the antisocial controls and a 22% increase compared to the normal controls. Liars had a 14.2 % decrease in prefrontal gray matter compared to normal controls.

Interestingly this isn't particularly seen as a deficiency problem, but more as an advantageous evolutionary shift.

"Lying takes a lot of effort . It's almost mind reading. You have to be able to understand the mind set of the other person. You also have to suppress your emotions or regulate them because you don't want to appear nervous. There's quite a lot to do there. You've got to suppress

All men are frauds. The only difference between them is that some admit it. I myself deny it.
(Jerome K. Jerome)

39

the truth. Our argument is that the more networking there is in the prefrontal cortex, the more the person has an upper hand in lying. Their verbal skills are higher. They've almost got a natural advantage. They've got the equipment to lie, and they don't have the disinhibition that the rest of us have in telling the big whoppers ...

When people make moral decisions, they are relying on the prefrontal cortex. When people ask normal people to make moral decisions, we see activation in the front of the brain ...

If these liars have a 14 percent reduction in gray matter, that means that they are less likely to care about moral issues or are less likely to be able to process moral issues. Having more gray matter would keep a check on these activities."

If these findings are replicated and built upon it could be of use to many different kinds of professional. Yaling Yang suggests, among other things, in the legal system they could potentially be used to help police work out which suspects are lying; in business they could assist in pre-employment screening, working out which individuals may not be suitable for hiring; and so forth. (So the new discrimination laws will not be about the color of your skin but the color mix of your prefrontal cortex!).

In their findings, the authors mention that separate studies of autistic children – who typically have trouble lying – have showed the converse pattern of gray matter/white matter ratios.

"The facts that autistic children have difficulty lying and also show reduced prefrontal white matter constitutes the opposite but complementary pattern of the results compared to adults with increased prefrontal white matter who find it easy to lie ...

Although autism is a complex condition and cannot be taken as a model for lying, these results ... converge with current findings on adult liars in suggesting that the prefrontal cortex is centrally involved in the

A man would rather have a hundred lies told of him than one truth which he does not wish should be known.
(Samuel Johnson)

capacity to lie."

(The other researchers were Susan Bihrle and Lori LaCasse, also of the USC College's psychology department, Patrick Colletti of the Keck School of Medicine of USC's department of radiology and Todd Lencz of Hillside Hospital's department of research.)

Although these findings are fascinating the samples are very small and some experts do not find them at all compelling.

Diana Fishbein, a behavioral neuroscientist at the Research Triangle Institute International in Raleigh-Durham, N.C[d1] has done work in

"an area of research about psychopathology in general and deception in particular. We are interested in what the neural substrates are for deception. It would be very interesting to know when someone is lying and how lying is manifested in the brain."

One of her studies found a major difference in the brain function of people who exhibited psychopathic behavior.

"Most people process higher-order cognitive function with the front of the brain and emotions in the limbic system, which is lower down ... Psychopaths treat emotional stimuli as if it was dry information, while cognitive information that includes rewards is processed in the limbic system."

The brain, which is the greatest processor of information in the known Universe, has evolved to lie in specified situations. For some people, as you may expect in an evolved system, this ability has gone too far in the face of our ethics. But it has implications for all of us as none of us will have the same white-matter/gray-matter ratio and research

A little inaccuracy sometimes saves a lot of explanations.
(Saki)

needs to be done to find out how the ratios play-out amongst the mass of us and if this 'ability' needs to inform us as we teach our children that fighting the wish to lie (in most cases) is the better course of action.

But, whatever further research proves, the truly challenging aspect of our ability, and the differing abilities individuals have, to lie, is the way in which we can lie to ourselves with utter conviction.

At the other end of the scale from pathological liars, are people who hold as an absolute truth something which is just a belief and who consider others wrong to disagree with them.

All ideas have evolved. These evolved ideas have their own survival rates. These evolutions can be tracked and are usually quite logical. Many people around the world would say today that polytheists were mistaken. Even Hindus who are routinely 'accused' of being polytheists because it has come to be seen as something less than monotheism, explain that their idols are the many differing images of one god who has an unlimited number of images. And not a few Romans and Greeks throughout the Classical period thought as much of their pantheon of gods as atheists do today, but for the believers 'at the time' it was an unshakable truth. In fact it was a truth worth killing for, worth dying for and demanding a certain public fidelity. This is how we usually treat truths. We get very confused with our ethical systems and we will kill for what we believe is true, as readily as we will kill someone we believe is wrong! If aliens had to describe humanity based upon our history that would be their first finding. A willingness to kill.

Liars need to have good memories.
(Algernon Sidney)

The whole idea of heresy requires an orthodoxy, and orthodoxies are limited to times and places and cultures. Like fashion trends when seen by others looking back into history or from another part of the world, they look strange, foreign, sometimes laughable and almost at times unimaginable. Who today would consider anywhere in the world, burning a baby to death as a religious imperative?

At the root of defining what a lie is, we must accept that, because of the way the human mind works, the extent of human knowledge is a key factor in our judgment of what constitutes a lie. So today we know that there no spirits living in rivers, but they were not sure about that at the time when they believed in Naiads. (Some people are not sure they don't exist even today). It is, after all, very easy to see a willfulness in nature's capricious waywardness. Lightning as gods fighting, floods as punishments, deranged behavior as demonic-possession etc., when you don't have a wider knowledge to have a better or even a different theory as to what these things are and why they happen. Especially when these things can kill you and so possess a very strong fear factor for human beings. We are informed by the nature around us - parrot gods were not created in the West because there were no wild parrots there. But when you are taught these ideas from childhood as part of learning how the world works, they take on a whole different meaning. Not merely part of our ideas of the world but part of our ideas of ourselves. Just as we have seen lying to others starts very young so too does lying to ourselves. Lying to ourselves is the skill that truly gets us through the days of our lives.

When someone said the stars were holes in the

Sometimes the lies you tell are less frightening than the loneliness you might feel if you stopped telling them.
(Brock Clarke)

firmament through which heaven's light shone and they knew they were just guessing, would that constitute a lie? Is a best guess a lie? Is a belief system a best-guess game? Perhaps since we now know there is no life without a sun, sun worshippers had it right all along - except for the baby sacrifice debacle.

As far as we know monotheistic thought is about 3,000 - 5,000 years old. Since human beings have had the same size brain in excess of 150,000 years, it would be my guess that there being a single creative genius (one god) was possibly thought about long ago but we will never actually know. When human beings began to settle and write down their belief systems the most ancient stories they told were of gods, spirits and meta-beings of many sorts, not a single god. But if you look at the road from polytheism to monotheism and see it as an example of reductionism, you can see how this is obviously the development of thought since starting with one god and developing into polytheism, is not a logical process. There is beauty in unity; not that outside of poetry, beauty is a good reason for believing anything. But merely that logic does have a definable beauty in its ability to describe great things in simple terms, and one god is obviously going to be a supremely powerful being, and supreme power appeals to the human gift for creatively designing unanswerable authority into our belief systems. We mirror it in our insistence in having one political leader at a time.

Belief systems are great stories but we all know stories are just that, stories - fictions to greater or lesser degrees. They are all based on fact - even the weird and wonderful world of children's writing in which I live doesn't have many fictional beings that are not in some way based on what

---

Lies are sufficient to breed opinion, and opinion brings on substance.
(Francis Bacon)

'living beings' are like. This 'fiction' nonetheless manages to exhibit lessons in truthfulness. Because as we find out more about the world we tend to leave behind mistaken ideas and thoughts ... those ideas are still in our history and mutate and still have a life with some people, but in the main ideas move our lying and our truthfulness on to new avenues. In this way lying and truthfulness are like a drama acted on the stage of the human brain. And who knows how many acts we still have to sit through. I doubt though many people would want to believe that belief systems exist because lies do, but it is interesting how we loop our ethics around our belief systems in a symbiotic relationship that we believe to be exclusive, but actually is not. It is possible to be highly ethical and not have a religion at all. It may even be preferable as having no god gives one supreme responsibility, as there are no get-out clauses of any nature.

There are many different explanations in belief systems about how the world was created. They cannot all be correct. But is it a lie to believe something to be true that isn't? Or is it just misguided? And given the fact that human beings are the most untrustworthy creatures on Earth is believing someone is watching you all the time not a sensible fiction to have people believe in? If CCTV cameras have lessened crime an all seeing-god must have some beneficial effect!

It is a shame that some sects believe they are 'right' and other belief systems are 'wrong'. To believe something that is only proven to yourself and to decry other people the right to prove things to themselves that are different, seems misguidedly selfish, even if it is very human. But it is a very human result of lying to oneself.

Lying is like alcoholism. You are always recovering.
(Steven Soderbergh)

STUART'S 'POKER-FACE' HAD LET HIM DOWN AGAIN.

If there is a god he's been playing hide-and-seek for the thousands of years human beings were ardent polytheists, and it's no fault of human beings if they think there are millions of him/her/it. The lies and counter lies in which people partake are part of the mixture of belief systems because some parts of all belief systems no matter how divinely inspired their believers say they started, are human creations. And, as we now know, human's have the ability to lie about anything if they can derive great comfort or get some 'handle-on-the-unknown', by doing so. Especially if they have reason to fear the unknown - after all would a powerless god who cannot

Lying and stealing are next door neighbors.
(Arabian Proverb)

look after all of us be one we would even want to believe in? What would be the point?

The addition to our beliefs about god, of ethical teaching (seen by some as the whole point of having a belief system) can only be because people lie to each other. As these belief systems see it,we need to tell each other the truth more. The whole idea that belief systems teach 'how to live' can only be because without them the founders of these belief systems were not that impressed by how people were living. In fact, deep in our subconscious selves, we may one day find that belief systems are a very human answer to the very human problem of the prevalence of lies. But then again ... we may not.

Self deceit (as we touched on above) gives one a system within which one can live in a sense of happiness. No matter what is happening in the world, that there is a god in some kind of overall control can be placed in this context. It is an engine for a certain kind of happiness or contentment. Much of religiosity (the structure, hierarchies and daily workings) of belief systems are designed to promote this contentment. To cement one's adherence and focus the mind. Which is why dissent and doubt are seen as enemies. Indeed heresies. And there can be no greater dissent than another belief system with its own structure and hierarchies.

It's part of the process of going back to that time as a child when someone else puts the food on the table, puts the table in the house, puts the house in the street ...

Isn't it strange that a lie (known or unknown) can actually provide a form of happiness? And maybe we lie a lot more than we need to or should, because we are striving

Every violation of truth is not only a sort of suicide in the liar, but is a stab at the health of human society.

(Ralph Waldo Emerson)

for those moments of happiness. Our belief systems have evolved along with us, as has our science, our ethics, our languages and everything about our thinking. And it should be expected that they would. For the whole of nature is about surviving and every religion since the dawn of our minds has had something to say about death. Why? Because it is the one thing we know we cannot survive. In the face of this, reason evolved belief systems, which have in them arguments for survival after death in one form or another. We appreciate embalming for the same reason, because it is easier to believe in a continued existence for our personalities if the body is more or less looking like it did when we lived. It is far harder to believe anything survives when grubs eat away the flesh and skeletons rot down. Hence the creation of the idea of a soul, because belief-systems have always been explanations of our experiences when we have had no other explanations to turn to. The soul being felt not seen, does not die.

But as Spinoza so brilliantly observed our 'experience' is wholly based in ,on and around nature. We know nothing that is not of nature and we cannot describe any god or gods without reference at all stages to nature. Therefore to all intents-and-purposes god and nature are one-and-the-same. Our belief systems are deeply entrenched attempts to escape this fact.

As we have surveyed forms of lies and touched upon the evolution of lying and what they could be used for outside of their immediate purpose, I shall spend the rest of this book looking at specific areas of lying: politics, business and war, and relationships. That is if you haven't burned it!

There are many other spheres I could have chosen as

You can fool too many of the people too much of the time.
(James Thurber)

in medicine, farming, law,etc. but for the most part the forms of lies never change from sphere to sphere and my choices are more than enough to give you adequate food for thought. Finally I will itemise research on how to recognise when someone is lying.

Sometimes I lie awake at night, and ask, 'Where have I gone wrong?' Then a voice says to me, 'This is going to take more than one night.'
(Charles M. Schulz)

49

In Politics

or
Evasion, Concision, Position

Machiavelli had it right. You have to be able to lie, kill and hurt without conscience in the short term, to be a leader capable of making millions or people you don't like do something they don't want to do. In fact he remained right up to 1939. After the Second World War leaders finally realized there is a 'community charge' we all pay for their lying on our behalf. But there are still many leaders today who seem to think they just have to sell you a story to maintain rule over you. And if their aim is to maintain rule, they are right because their authority rests upon a brilliance at population control (in its non-breeding connotation). I rather like the ex-Labour Member of the British Parliament, Tony Benn's adage 'I don't want to be ruled by anyone who wants to rule me.'

But one party states or dictators are not alone in their lies or in having a methodology upon which they base their lying. Knowing when to lie, to whom and for how long is one of the arts of politics. Actually, its probably become one of the arts of all and every career.

Although many of us have a democratic system which has taken thousands of years to develop, these days this system does seem to work on the basis I would describe as short-term dictatorships. Parties with fewer votes than another party can rule, parties in power have veto rights and

---

Lying rides upon debt's back.
(Benjamin Franklin)

can steamroller (and do) legislation through Parliaments.

Most political parties will lie about their true intentions when trying to gain power, and all do things once in power they specifically have said they would never do when on the hustings (raising taxes being the most common). We, the voters, let it go thinking we have pressure groups that bring these things to our attention and liberty groups to make enough noise when we need waking up. But in the main we seem to accept that if we take against a party, voting it out of power at the next election is punishment enough. This has naturally grown a sense amongst the political elites that elections are a form of sanction and they take it as part of the ups and downs of political life that they will lose power once in a while. So being in the opposition becomes as much of a power play as being in control. The only thing they really get upset about, are new parties threatening their power bases or, horror-of-horrors, making the voting system more democratic by making it proportionally representative.

This cosseted idea of politics leads intellectually different parties to do many of the same things in the wider political sphere. Parties will hide legislation in the small print, try to get away from bad news quickly and let good news out early to make the most of it. They bask in success and blame others for failure. They quell dissent in their ranks, retire difficult officials, buy off people they cannot get rid of who disagree with them (this is euphemistically called compromise), leak against people in their own parties who are 'rivals' (how can you be a rival if you all represent the people?), and a myriad other dubious activities none of which act in favour of either the electorate or the country.

No one can lie, no one can hide anything, when he looks directly into someone's eyes.
(Paulo Coelho)

Most important of all they ride tides of popularism attempting to dress themselves in the clothes everyone wants them to wear whilst underneath remaining just the same. (The best liars always seem to have a smile on their two-faces.) Have you ever wondered why parties are so similar? Your vote made them so. In fact leadership of any kind breeds lies because those who are led ask so many questions the leaders can never have well constructed answers to them all and if they tell the truth the led will lose confidence in them. Lies maintain the people's confidence and the people who are lied to, in the main, prefer to keep their confidence over being told the truth. We are back, at this point, to where lies give us a more comfortable view of life and, as far as I can see, this is the only reason for anyone to allow political lies to go unchallenged. For a political lie is a corruption and corruption unchallenged will only ever get worse.

Fundamental shifts come rarely and usually in an upheaval within the community. An upheaval so stark they are often termed revolutions even when not bloody. Politics is all about the status-quo because that is the path of peace and prosperity. But since prosperity itself relies upon an economic system that must always grow within a finite resource (the planet Earth) it is itself 'a fools' paradise' - even if those fools will be our great grandchildren and even if the crisis it will bring has taken thousands of years to come about. The system in which we are living and the planet Earth are on a collision course and no one will admit it. It would dent our confidence.

Politicians are able to lie to us because we lie to ourselves. Jobs are not as important as breathing -anything that harms breathing must be stopped. But as long as only a

---

No man lies so boldly as the man who is indignant.
(Friedrich Nietzsche)

few living creatures and a few fellow citizens stop breathing because of our prosperity, that appears to be O.K. Risk is a description of acceptable losses, not an ethical proposal. To lose one species on our watch would seem to be a misfortune, to lose thousands has to be deliberate carelessness. We would rather watch mass extinction than admit economics is a bad system upon which to base civilization.

Most of this tendency to lying, opacity and prevarication from leaders comes from the fact that no individual has 200 years to put anything right, we only have one lifetime and in democracies we don't even have that long, we have a legislative period of time between elections. This kind of pressure forces people to lie just to be able to get anything at all done. Filibustering takes many shapes and forms and long term planning is not structured into our systems.

How could one even begin to put generational changes into such a short term system? Well, we could begin by not allowing politicians to lie about it or we could demand long term agreements between parties before we elect them. We could create online forums to tell them what we want them to do and not wait for them to generate their own manifestos. Fundamental to this would be the consensus for the first time in human history, that stewardship of nature and not economics is the most important factor in politics. And the names of the leaders are meaningless. But we like economics. We like money. Its an extension of how we think and we are not evolved enough to do without it yet. Until of course, there is a stark upheaval. But even if one were on the horizon, for the sake of the status quo our politicians would never tell us.

The naked truth is always better than the best dressed lie
(Ann Landers)

If they can get through their few years of power, they know they can spend the rest of their lives blaming everyone else.

The task of leadership requires the leader, according to Machiavelli, to be publicly above reproach, but in private it may require immoral things to be done in order to achieve their goals. '**Their**' goals, not the people's goals.

In other words politics is the art of the hidden lie. Or as politicians term it - evasion or secrecy for the public good. Politicians have been lying like the rest of us since the age of four and 'negotiation' (the sine qua none of politics) is dependent on an intellectual play that drips out the truth slowly, if at all. Politicians are simply not being trained to be truthful and the structures into which they place themselves (political parties) are not inherently honest structures. How could they be? They have been created by a bunch of lying human beings.

Someone said when the Tory Party was created in the United Kingdom in the 1670s,

"A political party is little more than a conspiracy against the rest of the nation." (Quoted by C V Wedgewood: The King's War).

Excellent historian though she is, this quote is unattributed, but it is far too true across the world. A politician's lie is a personal conspiracy. But maybe every lie is an individual's personal conspiracy against those they are lying to.

Some people argue that a politician who has an affair should not lose their status because it's only sex. If that politician has an open relationship with their spouse I would agree with this, but if their spouse was lied to then it is correct that politicians should be brought to account. How can you even try to trust someone who lies to those closest to them?

One of the striking differences between a cat and a lie is that the cat has only nine lives.
(Mark Twain)

If they can lie to their spouse (whom they are supposed to 'love') they can lie to anyone. If they can betray oaths given in public (marriage) their word is proven to be untrustworthy. It is, after all, one thing to know we are being lied to and quite another to catch out the liar. Although four out of five lies goes unnoticed and shouting about the one we do notice might be considered ludicrous, to the political classes it is usually considered no more than bad luck.

There are many, many assumptions we have grown up with over the generations that were begun by people without our depth of knowledge. A country cannot be said to lie, but have you ever seriously thought of why we have countries, and is the existence of countries consistent with human behavior which we have now seen is a behavior that is 20% liar?

There were no countries before human beings came along. As we would assume everything we make reflects how we think and who we are, how far does the existence of countries reflect how we lie? Tribes fighting over their patch, languages which are basically different sounding noises referencing talk about the same things with a variety of idioms, have become gatherings of people all middling along in specific land-areas. I have the honor to live in a country that has created most of the countries on this planet because we had an Empire. Drawing maps was big business in the British Empire and redrawing them even bigger. So was breaking treaties because you cannot make an Empire without a lot of lying.

Of course legally countries exist - they have charters and sign agreements and peace treaties and set up border controls. We construct around us something we can get a

---

We lie loudest when we lie to ourselves.
(Eric Hoffer)

handle on in our reason because the Earth is too big an idea to be contained in the intellect of past leaders. Countries are part of the cultured lie we tell ourselves because they are the wall over which we are able to view other people. But actually, philosophically countries don't exist at all. That isn't saying much I agree, as philosophically nothing exists.

But it may explain why saying, God Bless America, doesn't actually work because God doesn't actually know what you are talking about. (This isn't an American bashing book, I just liked the subtle complexity of the joke.)

The sadness of the human construct of country is that countries will work against each other and there is no common thread anywhere in history where the human race has ever acted as one race nor will there be until we stop lying so much. Countries are a perfect vehicle to promote lies and give human beings, with already restricted vision, a cubicle all of their own. Whatever will these thinkers do when the Universe opens up to the human race? Plant flags everywhere?

Politicians have a simple problem. They want to be elected into power again and again. They can't tell people that it's an ego trip because the halls of power are a heady mix of moment and authority, so they tell them the 'country' needs them. That they are a safe pair of hands and that they know what they are doing for the 'country'. Funnily enough, the people believe them, so they keep saying the same things generation after generation. The country as a political construct has been with us for so long we can no longer define ourselves in any other terms. We even have passports which is the perfect way for others to control their view of who we

---

Oh, what lies there are in kisses.
(Heinrich Heine)

are.

If Pericles walked into the world today he would understand the lies the politicians were peddling. He invented a lot of them. (But he would be appalled at the mess the Greeks have made of the Parthenon.)

Of course lying to your own people is one thing, lying to other countries is de rigueur. Sir Henry Wotton said that an ambassador is a honest man sent to lie abroad for the good of his country (or, as he said it, in Latin - legatus est probus homo ad alias nationes missus ut mentiatur pro suae rei publicae bono).

Double-entendre's like this are a way of dangling a truth in front of a person without actually revealing it, and making them smile if they get it and annoyed if they do not.

The real problem seems to be that no matter what the subject, no matter what the time, human beings cannot agree about anything, which is why in a democracy there is not just one party, anyway. We all have our own agenda, and in that lies the cause of many of our lies. Because politicians feel they are right. We lie because we are right ... (but we don't want others to know it yet). This is why we have something termed plausible deniability, and why it is impossible to get politicians to give straight answers. They know that in their place, we would be lying too.

John Arbuthnot (a satirist and well known wit) writing in England in 1712, concluded that the people should be frightened by the French King at least once a year to keep them on message. Something the modern British press has taken on board with gusto. The history of Europe has been a history of Empire building, and competing Empires always

---

No man has a good enough memory to make a successful liar.
(Abraham Lincoln)

lie about each other. Lies to them are a useful weapon in the wider geo-political war.

Arbuthnot gives rules for political lying:-

They should be within the realms of probability (even a four year old knows that)

They should be varied (people who believe your small lies may well believe your big ones)

One should not obstinately insist upon a single lie (the more you repeat a lie the more likely it is it will be discovered)

IT SAYS HERE YOU SPENT TWO YEARS AS THE
SUPREME MASTER OF THE UNIVERSE?

A liar begins with making falsehood appear like truth, and ends with making truth itself appear like falsehood.
(William Shenstone)

Lies which promise or foretell something should not be repeated because they will be uncovered and speedily contradicted. (Brackets are mine)

In fact if you want to be a great satirist and wit too, sit down and work out which of your political parties are the greatest liars, when, why and how they have lied. It's a bit like shooting-fish-in-barrel but it has its moments.

The art of political lying is actually a game. (Arbuthnot and Swift published the tract The Art Of Political Lying, they had an alternative title in Greek which I won't bore you with.)

The game is easy. Take two players or more. Give them power. Tell them one of them has power over the other every four years. Put in a wild card player who has to ask them questions all the time (we call this player a journalist) and mark them on the inventiveness of their lies. The serious side to this game is that people get hurt. Politicians get people killed and destroy lives with their policies, (and note in English 'lies' is part of the word policies). But remember that is part of the acceptable 'risk'. There will always be losers and as long as their numbers are manageable it is acceptable. The political agenda is all that is truly important.

So, politicians lie to stop people knowing everything they are up to. Sometimes they say they do this because it's a question of national security, but the nation is only a human artifice. Nature really doesn't recognise countries and now sadly in a mirror image of nature, politicians no longer recognise lies. If they can give an excuse for it, it isn't a lie. The 'greater good' is the most prevalent excuse. For the greater good, their default position is to increase their powers

---

Pain forces even the innocent to lie.
(Publius Syrus)

of control over the entire population. Increase it until you are perfectly safe from the threats from everyone - except your own politicians.

But we are also to blame here. We like being lied to. We like being told taxes are not going to be put up. We like being told cheap labour is destroying our workforce. We like being told we can drive whatever we want, kill whatever we want, buy whatever we want. Lies pander to our selfishness and our world view. The view from our 'country.'

The truth ... that the world is finite and we have to have discipline and we cannot have everything we want just because we have buying power - reminds us of school. But politics is like a huge school. Our politicians teach us mathematics, economics and history. Every four years (or seven if you are French) they test our knowledge. When we elect them, we pass the test.

Jean-Michel Rabaté, Vartan Gregorian Professor in the Humanities University of Pennsylvania, published The Ethic of the Lie (2008). His focus is the American political scene but he points out:

"It is not that lying is more frequent in the United States than elsewhere, but, since the end of the Cold War, American culture has been polarized by this topic, finding in it an unlimited source of fascination, amusement, and horror. ..We lie quite often, four to six times a day on average..at the same time, we do hate liars, and even more detest being lied to."

It is a curious factor of human thinking that we lie to ourselves in order to bolster our personal world view. And I suppose we lie to others to support that same world view. It is a curious arrangement lies have with self-affirmation and even our self-confidence. I am sure those who think about the

So near is falsehood to truth that a wise man would do well not to trust himself on the narrow edge.
(Marcus T. Cicero)

theories of mind recognise this very well.

We accept lies in politics in much the same way as we accept them in every walk of life. Much as money is the oil on which civilization runs, lies seem to be the treacle we all wade through when dealing with other people except for the fact we don't go around licking them all.

Ok that analogy didn't work.

Mostly politicians lie because they couldn't get much done if they told the truth. It would be too difficult because the opposition parties would be able to shoot them down all the time. Politicians lie to each other and about each other. Presentation is everything. After all, when a politician lies if other politicians can't prove it's a lie, then why should we be bothered? It will all change in four years anyway. In fact there is only one political party anywhere in the world and we should just vote the Liars Party in.

There is a school of political thought that says the best politicians are those who do the things the people want them to do, but make the people think it is they, the politicians, who thought of it. I am actually a fan of the psychological approach to history but in the context of the present discussion, this would mean that it is our individual aims and objectives that successful politicians are matching. Look around the world, this is the sum of your ambitions.

And whatever happens, don't blame me. I didn't vote for them.

Of course I lie to people. But I lie altruistically -- for our mutual good. The lie is the basic building block of good manners. That may seem mildly shocking to a moralist -- but then what isn't?
(Quentin Crisp)

Conspiracies

or
I know I exist because crooks exist

In recent years, with the advent of the world wide web, conspiracy theories have rebounded out of the Dark Ages with renewed force and new attributes. Gone are the days when all you knew of the world came from priests and grandmothers. Thanks to the ease of getting graphics these days, each theory comes with its own coloured box, and images reputedly proving the theory with the seduction of colours, images and hyperlinks. If you want to be extra particular, people can clone headed paper and create quasi-censored secret material to make an authentic-looking official statement. Movies have imposed an unrealistic expectation on the abilities of secret services which, added to their real abilities, seem to make any absurd notion plausible. It all beats having to publish an entire invented book which would have taken weeks, if not months to write, as they did in previous centuries. Today, you can have you conspiracy theory outlined and detailed on the internet in hours, then farmed out though social media to hundreds if not thousands of people. You can run a blog with no other intention than to discuss them and have hundreds of thousands of followers. So pervasive have these techniques become they have been used with government sanction and have been able to influence mainstream political discourse.

And these theories often have credence, although they are lies.

The liar's punishment is not in the least that he is not believed, but that he cannot believe anyone else.
(George Bernard Shaw)

Why?

To begin at the beginning every psychologist ingenuously starts any discussion on conspiracy theories with the phrase 'they are nothing new.' So how old do we go? Were witch doctors knowingly selling gobbledegook? Were early kings as rapacious and cunning as modern kings? Are religious leaders willing their followers on with beliefs no one can objectively prove? When Descartes began to try to understand what existence actually is, he started by denying the existence of everything. Then he latched onto an idea and built up what he already knew of the observable universe from that. But for all his flawed logic, the thought experiment, 'how do I prove I exist?', is very instructive. Because all conspiracy theories emerge from certain uncertainties in the mind of the individual, just like all creation stories. And those uncertainties exist for us all. Even today, for science has proven we are insignificant in the universe and that insignificance affronts our vanity, which we usually call our 'sense of ourselves'. Thinking we know some things, yet being incapable of encompassing complete surety, is the life lesson we all come to terms with but, for some reason, some of us can't live with uncertainty. Nor can we hold opposing views awaiting resolution to come in the future, or not.

Firstly, most of these theories are credible. Not only to the credulous. There are cabals in history and attempts to falsify facts, or hide them, by people wanting to make money and those engaged in gaining power. Historians keep on uncovering new information on how growing numbers of people were controlled by their rulers. We don't have to

---

Lies are essential to humanity. They are perhaps as important as the pursuit of pleasure and moreover are dictated by that pursuit.
(Marcel Proust)

look to insurrections in modern countries and the ease with which governments tell everyone 'they are foreign inspired' to understand this. We need look no further than corporations who have extensively lied in their desire to make profits. The cigarette companies who knew their products were carcinogenic, decades before smokers were ever told, because they had the evidence in front of them. Edgar Hoover, the great patriot, who looked for any peccadillo in Americans that could suggest they were person's of interest while himself dressing up as a woman at home. Something that would have put anyone in a position of power on his radar. Leaders and celebrities have always been hiding 'something' from the public. Far worse than do as I say, not as I do. It is outright hypocrisy. It is also very dangerous for this lack of honest dealing with the people is one of the foundations upon which the credulity given to conspiracy theories, exists.

So, knowing this, everything we are told and everything politicians and leaders do is up for grabs as far as conspiracy theorists are concerned. If it sounds plausible, then they will be more inclined to believe it on the basis that the information is not coming from the government or offices of the government. We are lied to, they know it, what they don't know is how to discern the actual conspiracies from the invented ones. Have aliens visited the planet? Are they in concourse with governments and imparting modern technology to us? Is there an outside possibility this could be true?

Part of the problem is our willingness to hide things

There is nothing in the world more shameful than establishing one's self on lies and fables.
(Johann Wolfgang Von Goethe)

we all do from others. One of the first things psychiatrists say, and those tending to the traumatised across the board, is that the sufferer is not 'alone'. None of us are alone in our insecurity or uncertainty. But we don't all invent a world view to ameliorate the sense of loneliness and fear of being 'caught out' this leaves us feeling. We are all in a prison of some kind, whether social or psychological, whether financial or class, gender or physical. Whatever this idea of self is that is so hard to define and yet so obvious to experience, it leaves us open to suggestion.

Secondly, there is an unevenness of power in our societies. For the most part we are free to make money and spend money. Other freedoms are curtailed and most people feel trapped in our economic system. When you feel trapped but are told you are free, it tends to make you look for a truth you can accept and be skeptical of those telling you something that is obviously not true in your own experience. It is like telling a homeless person there are plenty of empty houses around. It is true, but it is irrelevant, unfeeling and ignorant.

Since there is no such thing as a universal truth, personal truth takes on a vital importance. The kind of importance that stops one from committing suicide or sinking into deep depression. These personal truths give you back some power. You are telling those whom you know are capable of lying, that you are not fooled by them. You then take the next step, and cease to believe anything they say and once you do that then every conspiracy theory becomes your playground. And the world view you begin to create has all the elements of

---

By a lie, a man...annihilates his dignity as a man.
(Immanuel Kant)

the actual world, but systematized into an organized series of orchestrated events. All outcomes have been planned, all policies accounted for, every step itemised and plotted. In such a world all wars are designed, all enemies fictional and all populations manipulated.

Thirdly, it is not always the powerless who hold such theories. A September 2020 Pew Research Center survey found that more than half of Americans have heard at least a little about QAnon, the complicated web of pro-Trump conspiracy theories that originated on the message board 4chan. In November 2020, two candidates who voiced support for QAnon theories were elected to Congress. There are also many anti-Semites in governments around the world, people who have immense power, and yet absurdly believe another people have all the power. These people are manipulators of mass thinking, what Dwight MacDonald would have called Mass-cult. It's a way of saying you know something others don't, but you are able to use those who ascribe to your particular theory to make money. All cults work in the same way. Conspiracy theory adherents are using the same exact parts of human psychology that all religions use - working on the imagination to create a world view from which those who created it directly benefit. Just look at the way Europeans slaughtered their way to Empires spouting goodly Christian intentions. Or the way Islam slaughtered its way to an Empire for the good of all humankind. It doesn't matter what the world view is or says, what matters is only, who believes it. President Putin of Russia knows this well but so does Boris Johnson in the UK. You have to keep your followers loyal

---

When a man lies, he murders some part of the world.
(Merlin)

PETS? OH NO, OF COURSE I DON'T HAVE ANY PETS MA'AM!

and so conspiracy theorists say the same thing over-and-over and if the rebuff is not robust, people will succumb to believing no one visited the moon, the Earth is flat, humans are descendants of alien visitors, Illuminati exist and that many of the hijackers of 9/11 are alive and well.

"... some psychological evidence suggests that people are drawn to conspiracy theories when they do feel uncertain either in specific situations or more generally. And there are other epistemic reasons why people believe in conspiracy theories as well in relation to this sort of need for knowledge and certainty. So people with lower levels of education tend to be drawn to conspiracy theories. And we don't argue that's because people are not intelligent. It's simply that they

You don't tell deliberate lies, but sometimes you have to be evasive.
(Margaret Thatcher)

haven't been allowed to have, or haven't been given access to the tools to allow them to differentiate between good sources and bad sources or credible sources and non-credible sources. So they're looking for that knowledge and certainty, but not necessarily looking in the right places." Karen Douglas, PhD of the American Psychological Association.

We all have your right places and our good sources. We also have rules of thumb, 'never believe anything you hear and only half of what you read' has been around for generations. These people are not unthinking. They are unable to discern the true nature of the world around them and find a status in the world view they feel comfortable in holding. Believing in a conspiracy theory at the lowest level, is like an animal making itself look bigger than it is in the face of a perceived threat. At the highest level it is a series of imaginative 'maybes' that enable theorists to overwhelm the imaginations of vulnerable people for their own purposes. Nationalistic, racist, genocidal … you name it we've done it. So, yes, there is massive danger in these theories. Revolutions don't happen in happy societies. Whatever 'happy society' means. The real conspiracies in the world, the Fascist movements of the 20th century, the East India Company of the 18th century and hundreds more, are a part of history. They have nothing to commend them

But the effort people put into these theories are so cemented in their world view they won't change them. You can tell someone who doesn't believe men went to the moon, that there are mirrors on the moon used by universities around the world to carry out experiments on time/distance/

Truth will lose its credit, if delivered by a person that has none.
(Bishop Robert South)

68

movement. Those mirrors were put there by astronauts. They will dismiss this. It is absurd that a fact can be ignored but they will ignore any and all of them, if it takes away their world view that they know something you don't, that they are fighting the good fight, that people are around who lie to them but they cannot be fooled. That power is used against the interests of the 'common folk' and that society is a battle of wits against titanic, dishonest forces. These forces are always other people usually in smaller groups.

People do lie of course, that is what this entire article is about. But in concentrating on theories others give them, conspiracy theorists miss the real ones. Media lie all the time, invention in the visual arts of TV and film are there to reinforce the imagination's conception on who we are and what our nation is. The oldest adage we have is that one person's freedom fighter is another person's terrorist. This is entirely true because none of us, as yet, have signed up to the same world view any more than we have signed up to the same religion.

"Conspiracy theories allow people to believe there is a hidden structure to the world. They are fundamentally reassuring – a comforting ideological fantasy – since they propose that someone, somewhere, is in control, no matter how malevolent they may be." Stephen Murphy and Tim Hill, Irish Times, April 30th 2020.

So we see that people allow themselves to believe in lies that give them a world view that provides comfort and/

With lies you may go ahead in the world, but you can never go back.
(Russian Proverb)

69

or provides answers. Exactly the same elements that created gods and a host of other superstitions.

"They want to believe in their cause and fight for their cause even if their rational mind tells them it's not something they believe in," says Carla Marie Manly, PhD, a clinical psychologist who specializes in fear, media, and the psychological impact of issues such as conspiracy theories on the psyche. "Sometimes, people get behind a theory because they agree with the underlying cause. We have this tribal mentality where we want to be part of a group," Manly says. "On a very primitive level, it makes us feel safe ... we feel like we aren't alone and part of something greater than ourselves where people understand us, and we understand them."

And underpinning all this is that we know there are real conspiracies out there. How many and where? And how much actual knowledge does it take to uncover them?

According to the leftist writer and journalist Upton Sinclair, in the First World War with the advent of air warfare, all sides made an agreement not to bomb each other's armament factories. Was this a conspiracy? From the ordinary solder's point-of-view very much so. From the general's point of view it was old-world gentlemanly warfare. There is no such thing as gentlemanly warfare. There is no such thing as ethical warfare, but there is such a thing as compassion within conflict. But that is down to the individual, not the armed forces. And this is something sociologists note and find hard to relay to people: individuals make different decisions than

Do not think you are going to conceal thoughts by concealing evidence that they ever existed.
(Dwight D. Eisenhower)

those made by the collective, given the same facts. The point about conspiracy theorists is that they are a collective. They won't all subscribe to the same theories but they all believe the world they are told exists, is filled with lies. Or perhaps we should say, liars. They are right. That's part of the problem, but they cannot discern a lie for a make-believe.

It has to be true that just as conspiracy theorists want comfort and to feel part of something bigger, so do most of us. Nations exist but they can't all be the greatest nation on earth. Sports exist but the amount of time and effort and funding that goes into them just so 'someone' can win 'something' is a ridiculous value system. But that need to be on a podium is actually in all of us. We live a vicarious life-style propelled to a sense of achievement through others and just as in Rome, sport is a sop to keep the masses happy. Even within families each person will be noted as being 'good' at something. And will get kudos for the same.

We are actually in a place where the normal work of governments is to conceal some or much of what they do. They tell us they do this to prevent our enemies from knowing what they are up to and to prevent opposition parties gaining the upper-hand on policy through foreknowledge. Democratic leaders throughout the world play this game and it plays into the hands of conspiracy theorists. Every policy becomes a smoke-screen to hide the hidden policy, statements become an art form to give away just what the party wants to give away and no more, and the desire for political parties to design the country in the image they and their followers want, becomes a to-and-fro game through election cycles. Until we are left

---

Lying to ourselves is more deeply ingrained than lying to others.
(Fyodor Dostoevski)

with the sordid saying 'who benefits from my believing this?' Tyrannies are even worse.

Perhaps, if we didn't lie to each other in our personal relationships we would be less likely to lie to those we lead. Here are some of the main issues over which people lie to each other in relationships according to some experts:-

About Career:-	Lovers lie about liking or respecting their partner's job or career. In an age when one's career can define a huge part of who we are this is tantamount to not liking your partner much.
A p p e a r a n c e / Health:-	Lovers lie about their age, weight, health, nose job and unexplained holes in their skin.
Attraction to Others:-	Lovers lie about their feelings and interest in others especially if they see those people regularly - such as work colleagues. They tend not to lie so much about desiring Hollywood stars but dress up as them in the bedroom.
Behavior/ Character:-	Lovers lie about liking their partner's habits, personality, hobbies, sense of humor. (I can't see those relationships lasting long there is nothing worse than marrying a bad comedian).

Mendacity is a system that we live in. Liquor is one way out and death's the other.
(Tennessee Williams)

Beliefs:-	Lovers lie about true feelings on important issues like religion, politics, their lover's companion animal, who holds the remote control and who their daughter really looks like.
Betraying Confidences:-	Lovers lie to each other about keeping secrets confidential. We love to gossip and when we don't, actually, we make it up anyway.
Career Performance:-	Lovers lie about how well work, school, their career is going, although if it's going very badly this is impossible to conceal from someone who knows your every mood swing. This is also allied to lying about money.
Commitment:-	Lovers lie about uncertainty or doubts they are having about the relationship. To admit any would start a long, involved argument - something many people want to avoid after a long day spent lying about their income.
Enjoyment:-	Lovers lie about enjoying things a partner likes to do. Oh, the misery of fun fairs.
Family/Friends:-	Lovers lie about liking other people who are important to a partner such as old friends and even family. None of us can help our relations - so be kind.
Feelings:-	Lovers lie about their true feelings towards a partner. Especially if the sex is good.

Please don't lie to me, unless you're absolutely sure I'll never find out the truth.
(Ashleigh Brilliant)

Financial Issues:	Lovers lie about their income, resources, inheritance, debt and spending habits. Not just because they may be self-conscious about them but because we are taught to conceal our earnings from everyone in case the tax man hears us.
Flirting:-	Lovers lie about flirting with strangers and sisters.
Time with Others:-	Lovers hide activities and time spent with others at fun fairs.
Infidelity/ Cheating:-	Lovers lie about having sex with other people and other people lie about how good it was.
Jealously:-	Lovers lie about being jealous and snooping and why they own packets of latex gloves that don't leave fingerprints.
Love/ Emotions:-	Lovers lie to their partners about feeling vulnerable or scared or deeply moved.
Masturbation:-	Men, in particular, lie about masturbating. I mean they lie about when, where, how often - not that they just lie about masturbating!
Past Relationships:-	Lovers lie about the depths of past relationships, as if past feelings are irrelevant to their present relationship.
Physical Appearance:-	Lovers lie about liking their partner's appearance, hair, weight, age, clothes and shoe collection.

Someone who knows too much finds it hard not to lie.
(Ludwig Wittgenstein)

Secret Contact:-	Lovers lie about intimate, but non-sexual contact with someone else especially if it's an animal.
Sexual Enjoyment:-	Lovers lie about how good sex with a partner is. If it is good they don't lie.
Sexual Fantasies:-	Lovers conceal having sexual fantasies about others during sex. Or thinking about sex with someone else unless its an agreed role play.
Sexual History:-	Lovers lie about the number of past partners, unsafe sex practices, what they have and have not done with others, their virginity, having an abortion, etc.
Sexual Orientation:-	Some lovers lie about same sex contact or interest.
Time Management:-	Lovers lie about being too busy, or have too much work to do or don't have time due to snooping and flirting, for whatever it is they are expected to be doing.

Just look at this list. Just consider the hurt engendered around the world in hundreds of millions of people because of them. In any other situation this would be considered a pandemic of lying.

Of course these are lies within some kind of normal relationship. There are relationships founded upon lies. Such people who set out to romanticize their own selves or give the relationship a romantic gloss for the sake of the romance,

---

I have a higher and grander standard of principle than George Washington. He could not lie; I can, but I won t.
(Mark Twain)

are not uncommon. If you want to be able to recognize such people here are some observations on common romantic relationship lies:

1. Romantic liars are very good at information control. If your partner knows far more about you than you know about them, there's a chance there's a hidden agenda in play. Evading questions about this is also an indicator. You have an idea of what your partner is like, but you've never really had any of the information verified.

2. Romantic liars make you feel like it's love at first sight, because the lying is designed to create intensity and a feeling that you are soaring through the air, in their arms.

3. Romantic liars have a built in need to keep their partners on a short leash and out of contact with people who might know the truth. It is common for romantic liars to go to some rather extraordinary lengths to limit contact with friends, family, co-workers, etc.

4. A lot of romantic liars present themselves as being more available than they really are.

5. Romantic liars lie about their educational background, their occupation, social connections, and so forth.

6. Romantic liars will often say they have a personal tragedy in their lives, losing a loved one, being in a disaster, etc.

I should like to lie at your feet and die in your arms.
(Voltaire)

7.   Romantic liars will lie about working for the secret service or being a specialist soldier.

8.   The internet is a great place for these people!

Are you wondering why in a chapter about conspiracy theories we started to talk about relationships?

In part it is because this list was in the original chapter 'on relationships' of the original essay, which I always thought was a cheap chapter. Who hasn't been lied to by a lover?

But the personal lies we give feed into the mass-cult lies we receive. It's a little like animal-cruelty, how can we ever talk about it without talking about war and what humans do to each other? So how can we talk about conspiracy theories without looking at the small, personal one-on-one conspiracies we play out with each other? If we can lie to those we are supposed to care about how can we not lie to the those we lead, and as long as those lies and secrets exist so will conspiracy theories.

The point about them is, to most of us, they appear absurd. The planes above our heads are deliberate giving off chem-trails that make the populations supine. That is ludicrous right? Then explain why, when facing an environmental crisis that could wipe out life-on-earth we don't all change immediately? Why do we look to governments to make all the decisions? Why do we just want to carry on doing what we have always done and not change? How can we be intelligent and not change?

If a lie is repeated often enough all the dumb jackasses in the world not only get to believe it, they even swear by it.
(Billy Boy Franklin)

Partly we can't, you need money to make changes and most people don't have enough. A few people think the whole climate change scenario is itself a conspiracy theory. Most of us though, just get set in our ways and yet others think wiping out billions of people is not a bad thing. To them humanity is a failed experiment.

And partly the science is so vast and huge we cannot conceptualise it properly. Can you see your bit of plastic floating in the oceans? Your car journey adding anything bad to what everyone else is doing? Your holiday making much difference to jet plane emissions? You see, as individuals we are so small and the problems so huge, how can any of us make a difference?

Conspiracy theorists don't subscribe to this laissez faire attitude. Give them their due they are mostly wrong headed, and absurdist in their views but they are certain,W structures in society are fake and need adjusting.

I wouldn't use the word fake. I would suggest broken. But they are broken because human beings lie all the time, about everything. That much the theorists have understood.

Make the lie big, make it simple, keep saying it, and eventually they will believe it
(Adolf Hitler)

In War And Business

or
The 36 Stratagems

Without lying there would be no wars and business would always be good. War is business by another name and business is war without the bloodshed - although in criminal business one should assume a certain amount of bloodshed.

Business and war even share a language. You can make a killing with a stock, have a tactical meeting to discuss take-overs, martial your defences against a hostile take-over, plan your advertising and growth campaign (propaganda), take-out the competition and so forth. In fact business people are probably all would-be generals - loving authority, following a certain discipline; even having an almost world-wide dress code. And if business is a pseudo-war carried out in offices and not on battle fields, and in electronic cyberspace, it is nonetheless true that in both business and war aggression plays a significant role and it is a very sad fact that war, for all the excuses we have for waging them, is and always has been big business.

If money making were taken out of the war machines of the world, and business was not able to subsume other businesses or erode the competition both would be shadows of what they are today in human society. If the great supply-and-demand chain, which hides a million crimes were

---

It takes a wise man to handle a lie, a fool had better remain honest.
(Norman Douglas)

shackled, civilization itself would be radically different, and in chaining our minds to business we become as single minded and dependent upon those around us as any soldier on any battlefield.

The Chinese thinker and warrior, Sun Tzu ("Master Sun"), also called Sun Wu, is traditionally considered to be the author of The Art of War, an immensely influential ancient Chinese book about military strategy. Strategy is the art of trying to outwit your opponent, an art in which, you can obviously see, lying would play a major role. This is also one of those areas where lying is usually considered justified because you are saving the lives of the people on 'your side'. However if you take the view, as I do, that countries are artificial constructs and people are the same everywhere, the narrow field of vision which makes warring possible is itself a fabrication which we all plug into. After generations of lies we have become very distrustful, and the putting up of barriers and walls is now second nature to us. This is not to say that we are not sometimes attacked and have to defend ourselves. This is an explanation of the rational that underpins the given reasons for the attack.

In fact Sun Tzu says that all warfare is based on deception and, in waging a war, one should be 'serene and inscrutable' (now those two go together). But before you dismiss him as some oriental thinker not relevant to the 'rest of the world' (and if you did - consider what you mean by world) bear in mind he was studied by Napoleon.

"In war, force and fraud are the two cardinal virtues."
Thomas Hobbes, Leviathan

I believed, therefore have I spoken: I was greatly afflicted: I said in my haste, All men are liars.
(Psalms CXVI)

All soldiers study the strategy and military campaigns of previous soldiers because there are rules on how to wage a war and prosecute a battle. And note that word 'rules'. Its one of those terms that in context hides an horrific amount, yet appears on the surface to be acceptable. It is acceptable because without some rules war is plain butchery. But even with the rules war is butchery. But the rules fool us. The rules tell us there is some ethical consideration in war. Actually true ethical considerations would make war the one action we would all work hard to expunge from the future of our endeavours. Except that we have an armaments' trade worth a fortune, practised by powerful countries. What leaders have ever suggested agreements to give that up?

Rules also saturate business. And most of them are there to restrict 'bad' practices and tell business people what practices are allowed and what ones are not. Reminiscent of the long and rather ridiculous arguments Europe had about waging a 'Just War.' Adulterating foods for human consumption saves money and extends profits but is considered unacceptable. Do you think without the rules and the power to back them up, people would never adulterate your food again? Of course they would because, after all, people are not to be trusted.

Business is so ready to lie to us we have to have a plethora of rules and regulations about what they can charge, when they can charge it, and what constitutes a sale of goods and what constitutes a bargain. We have to have safety regulations so that the things we buy in good faith won't kill or maim us, because - when all is said and done - business

---

When lying, be emphatic and indignant, thus behaving like your children.
(William Feather)

wants profit. Benefit to the community is secondary and has to be because without profit a business cannot survive. Entire communities can, and have been, sacrificed to the business of profit.

And even with all those laws we still need consumer groups to keep an eye on things. People will sell you things that will poison you if they can make money, and they do in parts of the world we have little interest in extending our safety regulations to. Things business people know kill, harm and poison are sold every day just as soldiers practice every day to kill harm and destroy and who knows - even poison.

Wars bring out the bravery and courage in men and women, but it is a fact that much of war is dissembling and falsehood. If it wasn't there would never have been an ambush. In fact only the Scots and Rajputs ever thought ambushes were a silly idea and it was much more to their liking to shout to their enemies and show what big swords they had. An act of true bravery is to go into battle playing bagpipes. It is also a great act of truth because it says we are here and we are coming. Sadly it cannot be said to be 'serene and inscrutable'.

Perhaps that is best said of the Gurkhas who fight at night and you don't know they are there until they are cutting off your head. Rather like a hostile business take-over where everything is done very, very fast on all fronts at once in the stock market, with the press and in the lawyers offices to make sure you have the best chance of success.

And after the take over you can dismember the other business and subsume into your structures what you want at your leisure. The legal framework of business empires, and the treaties of olden day Empires are not as different as you may

---

Splendide mendax
(Horace)

think. In the first place olden day Empires were predicated on the fact that owning more land made a country richer, and the writing of agreements (treaties) and the funneling of profits (trade) works for both.

Money seems to bring out the liar in so many of us one has to ask is it really the money, or just our natures? We hide the true costs to us of things we sell to others, we tell our workers we can't afford what we can afford, our workers try to get benefits without the boss knowing it, we sell things in less regulated countries we cannot sell to our own people anymore, knowing it may harm and even kill, we lobby governments, we bribe officials who enjoy the bribes, we even elect crooks to office. And when we have more money than we know what to do with ... we run for political power.

Happily, the rich don't lie to us, because they don't even talk to us. They just employ other people to lie to us; "This technology is safe." ; "This development is good for you." ; "Here is the data, here are test results."

It's all to make money out of us in new ways that have a strangely old feel to them. And worst of all business men and women believe they are doing the right thing for the community because the system is there to be made use of and they are keeping the system sound and in good order. The same system, mark you, that has wiped out thousands of species of animals and hundreds of native peoples running into million of individuals ... quite a price to pay for everyone to have a TV set. But I am sure many generals enjoyed it.

Talking about systems, we are told there is no such thing as a free lunch. Actually the correct statement should be: "There is no such thing as a free lunch within the system."

He who tells a lie is not sensible of how great a task he undertakes; for he must be forced to invent twenty more to maintain that one.

(Alexander Pope)

The monetary system was not and never has been, natural. There is an argument that war, in as far as it is aggression and counter-aggression, is natural. If true, money is either a way of channeling our aggression so as to create civil society or an unnecessarily aggressive way of creating civilization.

The Earth and everything on it is a free gift - it is human beings who cannot do anything without getting remuneration of some sort. Even the barter system depended upon an idea of mutual benefit. (War of course has no such idea unless the combatants are evenly matched and time and losses wear them down until they come to peace talks. Such peace talks are all about mutual benefit if no one has surrendered to convene them)

We are just not that community orientated to work for the joy of it yet funnily enough the whole economic system depends for its existence on the good will of everyone else. We make a small number of people rich simply by living and buying things in bulk. Without the rest of us, and the economic system we all adhere to, there could be no rich people-within the system. I mean you would still have famous people, and leaders and impressive thinkers but there would be no one on Earth who could grow rich by putting a price on originally free, natural resources and selling it to everyone else.

It may be our nature to be unable to build a civilization without money, but money is not natural. And economics being another of those structures with rules and boundaries that we plug into and love so much, enhances the ability we have to lie to ourselves. Many years ago extolling the virtues of Roman and Greek civilization I was told not to be so appreciative of societies that depended upon slave labor.

What does the truth matter? Haven't we mothers all given our sons a taste for lies, lies which from the cradle upwards lull them, reassure them, send them to sleep; lies as soft and warm as a breast!

(Georges Bernanos)

The enslaving and mass slaughter of animals underpins our entire banking system. Not much to extol in that.

Lying about the enemy and to the enemy is important in war. Commonly called propaganda in wartime and advertising in peacetime, its one and the same thing Camouflage is the most intelligent way people have ever thought of for saying, "Hey, we're not in."

It was a fact that in reporting losses and successes in the Battle of Britain the BBC doubled the enemy planes shot down and halved the British Air Force planes shot down. The reason for this was not, as has been suggested, to keep from the population of Britain how dire things really were, but to convince the listening Germans that the British couldn't count. And before you dismiss that as ridiculous, how much respect would you credit an enemy who couldn't count? (It is ridiculous though).

If you don't respect an enemy you will underestimate their intelligence. Lies in war do what they do in peacetime, they confuse and hide true intents and the true nature of things. Lies are a weapon and though we can see this clearly in wartime we should not be blind to the fact that, that is always their purpose. Between individuals they may often be a weapon of defence depending upon the situation and the lie, but they are still a weapon.

Even those lies people agree can be used, to withhold a painful truth from someone, are a weapon being used to defend either the person's feelings or the liar's situation. Aeschylus said that in war, truth is the first casualty. Deception can save your life and often your company (company, another one of those dual words that live in business and war. Engagement is

---

There are a terrible lot of lies going round the world, and the worst of it is that they're true.
(Winston Churchill)

one that lives in relationships and war but I am so not going to look at the similarities between war and relationships ... this book isn't long enough.)

Let it be said that as far as deception goes, there are many company directors out there grateful for having creative accountants.

People lie about stocks and shares and what's happening to companies, they spread rumors, they break the rules, they commit fraud and lie openly; all to take advantage of the ensuing situation and make money. (Rendering unto Caesar what is Caesar's is actually a divine suggestion that you

OK LADS, IT'S YOUR JOB TO MAKE THIS £30 BILLION DEBT LOOK LIKE A GOOD THING!

The difference between a saint and a hypocrite is that one lies for his religion, the other by it.
(Minna Antrim)

should lie at all times to tax gatherers - and it is heartening how many of us do).

Untangling lies to get at the truth can sometimes feel like a war. Ask any journalist or official receiver.

A business and an army are forms of human community dedicated to different tasks. Like other communities they are based on some assumptions about how people behave within their given task-set: that the community is formed for the benefit of all, that people are working to a common goal as well as to their own individual goals, etc.

Most people treated with honesty and concern will respond with loyalty and hard work. Fear, greed and patriotism can and are used by both these types of community but sometimes in a subtle way. In business, people are taught to fear 'being poor' and have instilled in them that this means being without an income. Is that true poverty? Or is that the definition of poverty within the system?

Lies in the business environment directly benefit the liars, in armies they can save lives which is of benefit to soldiers and generals. Which is ok, if it's your side's lies. Even soldiers know they don't know everything or see the whole picture but they do what they are trained to do as their part in the general effort. Exactly what individuals do in large corporations. Exactly what individuals do inside countries. The wealth of nations is, after all, a description before it becomes an ordinance.

Competitors are often treated as enemy armies are. Good business practice is to gobble up your competition if you can, large corporations are seen as empires, militating against your competitors (never give an idiot an even break)

Falsehood is easy, truth so difficult.
(George Eliot)

are all accepted practice. Why? Because the general public only like to see who is waving the flag and how much wealth/courage they have shown. How many lies have been told to get there is of no interest to them. See how angry people get when foreign owned companies buy their nationally known brands, or when they see people flaunting foreign imported goods. The word 'invasion' is not used much but the feelings generated by global business are much the same.

Perhaps this all reflects the internal war in us all, between truth and lies. Between being honest and telling lies. We wouldn't lie if the situation didn't force us too. We lie either because of our natures or because we are scared of what the truth might do to us. Although this is a comforting thought nonetheless we do take too much delight in some of our lies. And you won't find anywhere in business rules and regulations a simple rule, 'tell the truth all the time'. Business isn't like that.

It is well known that Goebbels used lies as a propaganda weapon. Propaganda is a kind of 'scientific lying'. Its purpose in wartime is to keep everyone in the dark whilst the war is being prosecuted and afterwards to leave such a net of confusion it's impossible to prosecute the generals.

Some argue that all persuasive communication is propaganda, while others suggest that only dishonest messages can be considered propaganda. Lets look at the dishonest side.

Harold Lasswell's broad interpretation of the term.

"Not bombs nor bread, but words, pictures, songs, parades, and many similar devices are the typical means of making propaganda ... propaganda relies on symbols to attain its end: the manipulation of

A giurar presti i mentitor son sempre. (Liars are always given to swearing)
(Vittorio Alfieri)

88

collective attitudes."

(H.D. Lasswell, The Theory of Political Propaganda)

Propagandists usually attempt to influence individuals while leading each one to behave "as though (their) response were (their) own decision." Mass communication tools extend the propagandist's reach and make it possible to shape the attitudes of many individuals simultaneously. Because propagandists attempt to "do the other fellow's thinking for him," they prefer indirect messages to overt, logical arguments. We do this by making calculated emotional appeals, by demonizing the enemy, by linking the war to the goals of various social groups, and, when necessary, by lying outright.

Businesses can be tremendously successful without engaging in fraud. While we may be fooled into buying products that are hyped, we also have a special affection for, and often a lifelong relationship to products we like. But all advertising and all propaganda has an angle and it is in that angle, that lies reside.

So effective was the propaganda in World War 2 that people even took against German breeds of dog. Now much as I loathe the Nazis and would see them as my natural enemy, I think it is ridiculous to think someone who owned a Dachshund was somehow unpatriotic. Actually, if they had read this book first, they would have been far more suspicious of people who bought Allied breeds and wrapped themselves up in the flag as if making a public display. The people one would have thought defined Britain, the aristocracy, were littered with fascists, and still are.

War and business can appeal to one's emotions,

Lies are usually caused by undue fear of men.
(Chassidic Saying)

denigrating the other side and appealing to the ends whilst passing over the means. The "War To End All Wars" is not far from, "The only cleaning fluid you will ever need". They are both lies. Objectivity is often difficult. We have employed lies to survive and have sex, to stem arguments and win battles, but now lying can actually limit our ability to reason clearly because we are not getting the information we need to make decisions about our lives. We all need to be far better at recognizing a lie when we are told one.

But that is so difficult when we are taught from an early age, even as our mechanisms for reasoning begin to take shape, to reason within the system.

(I am grateful to Dr.Aaron Delwiche,Associate Professor in the Department of Communication at Trinity University,Texas, for some of these observations).

Resolved to lie in the last dyke of prevarication.
(Edmund Burke)

Recognizing a Liar

or
An Um and an Itch

Be careful this chapter may turn you into a conspiracy theorist.

Have we come a long way in the last ninety pages? From seeing how lies start, how they are embedded in our mental abilities, to what extent they are taught and certainly how they are misused. Can we ever stop lying? Could there be a time when we lied 10% of the time ... or 5% of the time? Or is the habit, advanced by our natural ability, too ingrained? Perhaps we could, if we started to call each other out more when we hear a lie, but to do that we need to be sure. Sure that we are being lied to and sure that we don't mind having no friends!

Before you read this chapter you should have some idea in your mind of what kind of lies you want to know about and what kind you are indifferent to. If your best friend when asked what they did last night and instead of saying they were in place 'a' they say there were in place 'b' do you really care that much? You make the rules for your life. Of course if your girlfriend was in place 'a' it may make all the difference in the world.

It is impossible to always detect a lie but you can limit the odds. The work that has been done amongst jurors seems to show that contrary to popular belief, women are not much

---

To thine own self be true, and it must follow, as the night the day, thou can'st not then be false to any man.
(William Shakespeare)

better at judging when someone is lying than men. According to those trained in the police services about 4% of people are accomplished liars and they can lie very well.

In the following list please note if you are going to do jury service, don't pay the items any attention. You will not be conversant with a body language that is culturally different from what you were brought up to understand and potential indicators of lying are also indicators of natural stress, illnesses and psychological problems. I wouldn't want you to find the innocent guilty because of this little book.

Liars are not just poker-faced, they are as expressionless as humanly possible (if they are not people simply suffering from Mnbius syndrome.) Bland and restricted they move their arms and hands rarely and when they do, movements tend to be inwards, towards their own bodies, as if they were trying to take up less space than usual. Few liars are effusive in their lies. What movements there are may be are off-timed and inappropriate (frowning at a piece of whimsy, smiling at a serious rejoinder, for example.)

Liars nearly always avoid eye contact. Even introverted people will glance into your eyes once in a while whilst talking to you, painfully shy people will look down, but liars actively avoid eye contact and look down and blink less (some sociologists say this is a misconception as lies are so habituated the liars don't even think about them as lies so are not abashed at using them.)

Telling lies is a fault in a boy, an art in a lover, an accomplishment in a bachelor, and second-nature in a married man.
(Helen Rowland)

Liars will touch their face, throat & mouth as they talk. They will scratch their nose and/or behind their ear. Remember they may do this even when they have told the lie and stopped talking. The lie 'lives' while the conversation continues. It also comes back to haunt them - we hope.

Liars will change the pitch of voice or rate of speech (this can also be a sign of singing).

Liars displays of emotion may be delayed and when they arrive, stay longer than natural.

Liars very often preface everything they say with an exaggerated, "Uh ...". Beware of the person who responds to every one of your queries with "Uh." Men do this more than women. (Uh, um - how many politicians have you heard doing that?) This will be especially true of most lies as they are given 'in the moment' and off the cuff. Practised liars with their planned lies will be fluent. So in effect politicians who 'um' a lot are not practised liars. How comforting.

A liar gets defensive if challenged. An innocent person will often go on the offensive. In fact, challenging someone you think has lied is often a good way of proving it. Taking them by surprise will make them have to say something more rapidly than they can think it out. The unexpected questions, as interrogators term it.

We lie loudest when we lie to ourselves.
(Eric Hoffer)

HOW MUCH WOOD WOULD A WOODCHUCK CHUCK,
IF A WOODCHUCK COULD CHUCK WOOD?

A liar is uncomfortable facing the person they are lying to. If they are lying to a lot of people at once this is shown by the fact they look around the room not catching anyone's eye, and even turn their body away. This should not be confused with teaching.

Liars might unconsciously place objects (book, coffee cup, etc.) between themselves and you. This is part of their instinctive defence but it does rely on how serious they consider their lie to be. Saying your phone was out of order when you didn't pick up, might not be a big lie. Saying you paid with a larger amount of money than you actually did, so the retailer gives more change might be seen as a big lie, in which case an entire counter is placed between the two of you as a cup would not be sufficient!

A liar will mirror your own words to make answer to a question. When asked, "Did you eat the last cookie?" The liar answers, "No, I did not eat the last cookie." It's almost as if they are learning to speak your language.

A liar wants to go. They may end the conversation unexpectedly and lie about why!

You can fool too many of the people too much of the time.
(James Thurber)

A statement with a contraction is more likely to be truthful: "I didn't do it" instead of "I did not do it." A liar tries to be subtly emphatic. If you think the liar is convinced of the truth of their statement, you are more likely to believe in it. This goes wider into the 'use' of language as it is perfectly true that good orators know many tricks and people untrained in oratory can be carried away by the sentiments and use of language and barely see the wider picture. Impressive dictators usually have excellent oratorical skills. Their ability to tell the truth (if they have it) is often less well practised and less needed.

Liars may not make direct statements. Their answers may be implied so you cannot come back at them with their own words later and tell them they are cheap. They can respond that you misunderstood them and there was no lie given. Many years ago I went to hire a room in a college of which I was not a member and the Don asked me, "Are you a student here." I knew he meant of the college but I took it in my apology two days later, that he meant the University itself (when you study linguistic logic this kind of dualism in meaning in common-place.) He accepted my apology and for my lie I didn't get to hire the room. We still had the party.

If one is to be called a liar, one may as well make an effort to deserve the name.
(A. A. Milne)

Liars can be garrulous, adding unnecessary details to convince you, they are simply not comfortable with a silence or pause in the conversation. Maybe because they don't want you to have the time to figure out what they have said is a lie. Since most lies are given at the spur of the moment, sometimes for unthought-out reasons and reasons even the liar cannot explain except maybe to keep in practice, they are unsure of the logic and whether it all hangs together. Liars want the conversation to be well and truly over.

However, bear in mind, an excellent liar adds effective details. Anyone who watches Kevin Spacey's brilliant near-last scene in The Usual Suspects will understand how persuasive this can be. This takes a high level of intellect and it is a fact that more intelligent people can lie effectively to less intelligent people. They can also talk down to them which is annoying because it is not a sign of intelligence at all.

A liar may leave out pronouns and speak in a monotonous tone. When a truthful statement is made the pronoun is emphasized as much or more than the rest of the words in a statement. I simply don't know what comments I can make about this. If it is true, then some very small words in English have the same affect as sodium thiopental. At least that is what I intend to tell anyone who suggests I need interrogating before they allow me into the United Sates for my book tour.

As one knows the poet by his fine music, so one can recognize the liar by his rich rhythmic utterance, and in neither case will the casual inspiration of the moment suffice. Here, as elsewhere, practice must precede perfection.

(Oscar Wilde)

A liar's words may be garbled and spoken softly, and syntax and grammar may be off. In other words sentences will likely be muddled rather than emphasized. A bit like telling a story as you go. This of course is most pronounced in a lie that is quite long. Which is why we like our lies to be short and swift, like our affairs.

If you have a gut reaction that you are being lied to, you might be picking up on micro-expressions which last about a 25th of a second but are indicative of a concealed emotion. These are the same kinds of expression as normal, frowns, smiles etc. but so fast the eye barely picks them up but the brain nonetheless registers their passing.

Making contradictory statements that just don't hold together should make you suspicious someone is lying (or drunk).

All lies and jests, still a man hears what he wants to hear and disregards the rest.
(Paul Simon)

Look for inconsistencies with the way things usually are. The world works in a certain way and oddities should be taken into account - except in England, home to great eccentricities, where oddities should be taken with a pinch of salt. You want to pay attention to someone who is generally anxious, but now appears calm or vice-versa. This supposes that you know the liar quite well. Amongst those who train liars (yes, they exist) having as little contact with your victim (the lyee - and I am so hoping this new word does not get into the language) is recommended for this very reason. You would think relationship lies could not happen as much as they do if familiarity breeds perception. Perhaps, as we noted above, we deliberately give people we know more rope because we don't want to believe they could lie to us.

Liars take advantage of the situation. It will be easier to lie in an e-mail than face-face. It will be easier to lie in passing than in a long, drawn out conversation. It will be easier to lie if you are strangers. Situations in which you know lies ensure may be: have you just arrested them? Are they appearing as witnesses for the Defence? Are they your lawyer? Are they selling you something?

Low self-esteem, depression and drug addictions are associated with compulsive lying. So you should show compassion to these liars but not weakness.

Now remember, a good actor is supposed to be able do the overwhelming majority of the things on that list with

---

Liars are the cause of all the sins and crimes in the world.
(Epictetus)

conviction. If you recall the chapter on children you will remember that all lies are told to manipulate a situation in the liar's favour, or at least to the disadvantage of those being lied to. So one question you could always ask yourself if you suspect you are being lied to is; who benefits from my believing this? It is a very useful question.

Most thinkers who have approached the topic of lying tend to think some lies worse than others (those saints again) and the situation in which the lie is given is a mitigating factor. We read an impartial, incomplete list in chapter one. Taking this a stage further experts have concocted a list of the types of liar. Within any circle of friends when you gossip about each other I am sure you will have come across these kinds of liars:

Occasional:- This is most of us and this is where we fidget most. We do this to avoid any unpleasantness, we don't lie a lot, we don't even like lying, but yet we do. It is not impossible some of them will be big lies but for the most part they are probably small lies.

Frequent:- The other end of the scale. They are not uncomfortable lying but because they do it a lot they often make mistakes in their sequence of events within which they have couched their lie (or maybe they are drunk a lot).

Lying is done with words and also with silence.
(Adrienne Rich)

Habitual:-	Habitual liars are fairly uncommon, at least in the United Kingdom. These are people who have difficulty separating fact from fiction. But catching them out is like shooting fish in a barrel and depends only on whether you feel it is worth your time. For them it's just a hobby.
Popular and Unpopular:-	Some people we enjoy lying to us. Storytellers, magicians and other entertainers who fool us with their work. Some we don't enjoy but we still let go like politicians who end up with titles and immense wealth for a life-time of evasion (and sometimes invasion).
Professional:-	These people plan the details of their lies and even rehearse answers if you catch them out on a particular statement. They want their lies to work and will refine them by using them on different people until they work well. They not only include people selling you something, they also include con-artists and crooks and 'modern' art.

There is no lie that a man will not believe; and there is no man who does not believe many lies; and there is no man who believes only lies.

(John Sterling)

Delusional:-   These people want their lies to be the truth (a lot of charlatan practices fit this category). They are mostly lies about their circumstances or background or position in their workplace.

Fibbers:-   I am including a category for those people whom we don't want to call liars. Usually aunts. They have wonderful stories and inventions but they never mean to harm anyone, anytime, anywhere.

Sociopaths: Of course these people will lie. They are manipulative, often quite callous, shallow, lacking in guilt with a tendency to criminality to lesser or greater degrees and often have an inflated opinion of their own worth especially when set against the worth of another individual. Probably you dated someone like this at some time in your life.

In every generation we have tried to catch out lies, some great, some smaller, some huge. Some history has been made because of lies and some lies are lost in the mists of time.

Indeed if a lie comes to be believed, it has all the hallmarks of truth so does it really matter any more if it is false as we cannot prove it one way or the other? We still base a lot of our civilized expectations on thousand year old assumptions that were made by men and woman who

---

It is easier to believe a lie that one has heard a thousand times than to believe a fact that no one has heard before.
(Anonymous)

did not have the same view or knowledge of the universe we have today. And in a hundred years that knowledge will be even greater if we are all still here, and who is to say our assumptions today will not appear absurd to our great grandchildren?

How many people still believe animals have no languages or feelings? How many people go out with precision guns and shoot herbivores from cover and call themselves hunters instead of killers? How many people believe a city to be a great monument to human design instead of a breeding places for disease and, in effect, a giant bank? And how many of us still believe nature is to be conquered more than loved? So many of the lies we live by have come from ancient people who believed them to be true, we have no such excuse. We have come to lie so readily we have begun to believe our own lies.

At the very least its great material for cartoonists.

If we have a natural ability to lie it is still true that we are taught how to use it. However, those first lies which we use as children to help and which have no malicious intent, become malicious as we grow up. We use lies to protect ourselves and when we are protecting ourselves from harm or death it is considered just. But an ability that is 'just' in extreme cases, like so many of our abilities, crosses different lines in our view of ethics when we use them in casual, everyday circumstances. We have come to the place where some thinkers suggest if we started telling the truth, civil society would break down in a single day.

The question arises again and again as to why we accept being lied to by those around us: by advertisers, by politicians, by business people, by those we love? And we do

A truth that's told with bad intent beats all the lies you can invent.
(William Blake)

accept it and what is more we lie back. It is true enough that lying has helped us survive against an antagonistic world and even worse, antagonistic people, but what helped one million people survive in a single city two thousand years ago, has become ingrained in our global, six billion large civilization.

We are at that point in our global civilization, everyone reaches in their own relationships, when lying is detrimental to the survival of that relationship.

We are actually at the point where truth will save us. Where honesty will breach our natures and marry our reason to our values. There is nothing stopping us being more transparent except some residue fear that somehow being honest makes us vulnerable.

We have spent some time looking at politics, relationships and warfare and business. Its an eclectic mix. We could have chosen other spheres such as education and medicine. In medicine the noble lie is most profound because it is here that time and again lying to someone who is dying to save them pain, or stem a suicide attempt, is repeated by ethicists down the generations as being an ok lie. However if the patient is also a doctor it is useless to lie to them because they know what you know.

And if you come away from this book with a smile and nothing else remember that lesson. If you have as much knowledge as the liar you cannot be lied to. Knowledge is your path to truth. Liars depend upon your ignorance.

And that little bit of wisdom is worth remembering.

Almost the End

Lying is an indispensable part of making life tolerable.
(Bergen Evans)

NOW BE HONEST... YOU WEREN'T ENTIRELY TRUTHFUL IN
YOUR PERSONAL ADD WERE YOU!

Calvin Innes

UK COMIC
BOOK ARTIST,
ILLUSTRATOR,
CARTOONIST
& ANIMATOR...

✉ mail @calvininnes.com
☎ 07760427798
🌐 www.calvininnes.com